I0152570

VITAL FORCES OF
THE EARLY CHURCH

BY

H. A. A. KENNEDY
D.D., D.Sc.
NEW COLLEGE, EDINBURGH

WIPF & STOCK · Eugene, Oregon

Wipf and Stock Publishers
199 W 8th Ave, Suite 3
Eugene, OR 97401

Vital Forces of the Early Churches
By Kennedy, H. A. A.
ISBN 13: 978-1-5326-1883-3
Publication date 3/10/2017
Previously published by Student Christian Movement, 1920

PREFACE

THIS volume is entirely due to the conviction urged by the officials of the Student Christian Movement, that there was room for a treatment of the earlier growth of the Church which should give prominence to its inner forces rather than its external history. I know that, regarded from this point of view, the treatment runs the risk of lacking in concreteness. But the attempt seemed worth making, although no one is more conscious than I am of its defects. I have at least tried to go to the sources, and to make no general statements for which authority could not be adduced.

My warm thanks are due to Messrs J. R. Coates, B.A., and Hugh Martin, M.A., for the kind interest they have shown in the preparation of the book, and for the real trouble they have taken, by supplying questions for discussion in study circles, to adapt it more fully for practical purposes. To them I am also indebted for various suggestions in the references to available literature, as well as for valuable hints towards the entire shaping of the discussion. Mr Martin has been so kind as to prepare the index.

H. A. A. KENNEDY

NEW COLLEGE, EDINBURGH
June 21st, 1920

CONTENTS

VITAL FORCES OF
THE EARLY CHURCH

CHAPTER I

INTRODUCTION

Matt. v. 1-20 ; Acts ii., iii., iv., v., vi., vii.

No more fitting summary of the account given
in Acts of the Early Christian movement
could be found than the words of chap. xix. 20 :
" So mightily did the message of the Lord
grow and prevail." The book intends to be
a narrative of the victorious progress of the
good news of Christ. Even those elements in
it which fail to appeal to us were influential at
the close of the first century A.D. This was
what Christianity had achieved. It had come
to occupy successfully the chief centres of the
ancient world. It had spread from Jerusalem
to Rome.

We have a picture of the methods of its
progress. These methods are bound up with
prominent leaders. Such emerge, in the first
days, at Jerusalem, from among the members
of the Twelve. Peter and John are marked
men. No less so is James, the son of Joseph

and Mary, who apparently associated himself
with the new Faith only after a remarkable
experience of the risen Jesus (1 Cor. xv. 7).
The part played by St Peter in the first half of
the book gives place to that of St Paul in the
second. There the author speaks from direct
personal acquaintance with the facts. Were
these men of unique eminence ?

It is futile to talk of the Apostolic leaders as
ill-bred, uncouth, illiterate men. That estimate
is due to crass explanations of such passages
as Acts iv. 13. It was their religious earnestness and spiritual penetration which had
prompted them to follow Jesus. The two
years or so which they had spent in His
company must have brought the profoundest
kind of education. Spiritual illumination is
life-enhancing on every side. It constantly
affects the intellect as truly as the emotions
or the will. These apostles must have shone
in any society. Jesus seems to have recognised that in sending them forth as His
delegates to evangelise Palestine several years
before. He never doubted that they could
take their place wherever they went. Their
equality in the early community with men
like St Paul reminds us of their unusual natural
equipment.

But, difficult as it is to reach a full interpretation of the opening chapters of Acts, it
is plain that after the first believers became
convinced of the undying life and supremacy

of their Lord, they attained a new level of spiritual endowment, called in the documents "the gift of the Holy Spirit." The risen Jesus is represented as having prepared them for this (Acts i. 8). And Peter, who seems to speak quite calmly, has no hesitation in referring to the ancient prophecy of Joel (Acts ii. 16 ff), which connects with the coming Messianic epoch such a special visitation of the Spirit of God.

It is interesting to note that Joel speaks of the unique gift in terms of prophecy. No adequate explanation has ever been given of *prophetic* phenomena. Whatever else was involved, an unusual religious receptivity was presupposed in which the human spirit was turned aside from earthly and material interests. It became deadened to the secular, and marvellously alive to the Divine. Philo, who had long reflected on the meaning of prophetic inspiration, thus appeals to the soul : " Go forth from thyself, filled with a Divine frenzy . . . and holden by the Deity after the manner of prophetic inspiration. For when the mind is filled with God and is no longer self-contained, but rapt and frenzied with a heavenly passion and driven by the truly existent and drawn upwards to him . . . this is thy [Divine] inheritance " (*Quis Rer. Div. H.* 69-70).

The main effect of this remarkable experience was a new sense of spiritual *power*.

It was inevitable that in the late traditions
embodied in Acts the power should be
associated with miracles and marvels. But
any penetrating reader can discern that what
really counted in the primitive community
was the abnormal endowment for spiritual
situations. So that it is not going beyond the
evidence to say that the early Christians soon
began to feel their call to victory. From their
intimate knowledge of Jesus they believed that
this was the Divine purpose. Hence they
never hesitated to become fellow-workers with
God. The outcome of this equipment in their
daily thought and feeling was enthusiasm.
So much is plain from the opening chapters of
Acts, corroborated by many passages in
the Epistles. It is unfortunate that attention
has been turned aside from the more general
features of the community to such more or less
accidental details as the sale of their goods
by individuals and the contribution of the
proceeds to a common fund. The important
feature in the famous story of Ananias and
Sapphira is not the terrible penalty represented
as falling upon them suddenly, but the high
standard of Christian morality which the
story presupposes.

Already in Acts, we see the spread of the
Christian mission, not only among Jews but
also in the Gentile world. This necessity
followed from the circumstances in which the
new message was proclaimed. We can hardly

doubt that the first envoys of Christianity to pagan society were to be found among those Jews of the Dispersion who had retained their loyalty to their faith : who travelled up to Jerusalem to perform the prescribed rites ; and who, as we learn from Acts ii., were brought into contact with the religious enthusiasm of the disciples. Nothing would impress them so forcibly as what the new Testament calls "the glad fearlessness" ($\pi\alpha\rho\rho\eta\sigma\iota\alpha$) of the Christian society. This was truly a notable characteristic. These first disciples were far from being self-assertive. They did not thrust the experiences which had transformed their own lives upon their fellow-countrymen. Nor did they display moods of pride and self-satisfaction. But they felt they were living under changed conditions. The rank and dignity which had commanded their homage ceased to tell in any practical fashion. They rejoiced to obey God rather than men (Acts iv. 19, 20), although they might have put forward mighty claims. They had discovered as never before that "the earth was the Lord's and the fulness thereof" (Ps. xxiv. 1). They accepted all His mercies with unmixed thankfulness, recognising that now they understood the meaning of life. And the keynote of their dispositions was joy. I doubt whether we should assign any definite set of causes for this. It was really due to the new value which had been imparted to all things, that

new value formulated by Jesus Christ.
Perhaps its real meaning may best be understood from the recurring phrase in Apostolic
salutations : " Grace and peace from God the
Father and our Lord, Jesus Christ." The
mind which sincerely felt like that was possessed
with a superhuman satisfaction.

It is clear, as we might expect, that this
extraordinary movement had its birth in
Judaism. This was no mere accident in the
Divine government of the world. Where else
could Christianity have found itself at home ?
By far the larger part of what was permanently
valuable in the religious heritage of the race
belonged to the Jewish people. No other
nation had shown itself so growingly sensitive
to the idea of God. No other had been
similarly trained by experiences of prosperity
and despair to know its own inner life, and to
recognise the eternal principles of moral aspiration. No national history could present
the same varying record of fear before God's
anger and delight in His favour.

Jesus, who was born a Jew, received a great
share of His nurture from the study of the Old
Testament. Nowhere else could such a
collection of fresh and living thoughts on
spiritual things be discovered. It does not
seem to have been the Founder's purpose to
cut loose His society from the real privileges
into which its members had been born. He
had come, not to destroy, but to fulfil. Un-

doubtedly His idea of fulfilling was most drastic. It meant the casting aside of what was obsolete, as having done its part in the spiritual training of the people. It meant a wholesale correcting of the points of emphasis in the religion of His day. But Jesus does not seem to have feared confusion between Judaism and His own purified faith. " Let both grow together " : that was His general attitude. A day must come when the new wine of the Kingdom should demand new bottles. He left all decisions of affairs to the wisdom of those men whom He had educated to carry on His work.

Obviously it was of primary importance that for months, if not years, the new movement should have the benefit of the protection given to Judaism. There was much consolidation to be done. The young Christians must learn for themselves that they were starting on an adventure without parallel in the history of humanity. They must gradually be prepared for misunderstanding, obloquy, persecution, even death. They must come to realise that claims such as theirs had never been tolerated by any power. They must be ready to " count all things but loss compared with the surpassing excellence of knowing Christ Jesus their Lord " (Phil. iii. 8). In all likelihood they never definitely deliberated on the situation, but rather let events lead them onwards.

Stephen's address is one of the most remarkable symptoms of change. The Jewish authorities might well suborn witnesses to procure his downfall. For the positions he occupies show that he had perceived much of the hollowness and futility of existing religion, and that he had gone far to grasp the teaching of Jesus: "God is a spirit and they that worship Him must worship Him in spirit and in truth. For the Father seeks such to worship Him." We need not be surprised that Stephen's words and Stephen's fate created a profound sensation at Jerusalem. They must have convinced the spiritually sensitive among the followers of Christ of the inevitable inference from their position. And no less powerfully must they have drawn the attention of the Jewish authorities to the humble group of men and women who preserved alive the name of Jesus of Nazareth.

A bitter persecution against the community is said to have arisen, which drove its devoted adherents in all directions. Perhaps its most important feature was the fresh impetus given to the zeal and bigotry of Paul. With his entrance upon the scene, the most famous moment in the history of the early Christian Movement has been reached.

QUESTIONS FOR DISCUSSION.

1. What were the chief characteristics and qualifications of the apostles ?

2. What is the significance of St Peter's quotation from Joel on the day of Pentecost ?

3. What is the relation of early Christianity to Judaism ?

FOR FURTHER READING.

The Book of Acts. By J. Ironside Still.

Christian Life in the Primitive Church, pp. 1–80. By E. Von Dobschütz.

History of the Christian Church in the Apostolic Age, pp. 64–112. By A. C. M'Giffert.

CHAPTER II

EQUALITY

Acts viii., ix. ; Gal. iii. ; Eph. ii., iii. ; Col. i.

WE are not here concerned to give any sketch of this all-important figure. It is difficult to say whether the early Jewish Christians were able to estimate St Paul's powers. In any case, for a time, he showed himself their most formidable opponent. But the persecution which he led had the effect of diffusing the new outlook. Probably it was of the utmost value that he pursued his path so whole-heartedly. His zeal must have been one of the influences which prepared a Church in the Diaspora. At any rate, to quote Acts viii. 4, "they that were scattered abroad went everywhere preaching the word."

The effect of his conversion to be a missionary of Jesus Christ cannot be overestimated. No wonder that Ananias at Damascus hesitated to approach him. No wonder that his Jewish hearers in the Damascus synagogues were doubtful. No wonder that finally the Jews of Damascus "took counsel to kill him." All of them were aware of his pre-eminent ability and of his unflinching conviction. It was an extraordinary gain for the young movement to make such a convert. No one was better aware of the weaknesses of Judaism than this Pharisaic expert. No one was more alive to the needs of the Diaspora than this brilliant native of Tarsus. He was equipped with the best that a scribal training could give him, and yet he had surrendered all for the sake of the Christ Who had laid hold of him. We shall have occasion again and again to emphasise Paul's unique importance for the Early Christian Movement.

At present let it suffice to concentrate attention on his epoch-making discovery that Jew and Pagan met on the same platform in Christ Jesus. I am fully aware that this is a platitude for our thought. It seemed an incredible paradox to that early world. We catch the Apostle, in his maturer years, speaking of it with bated breath (*e.g.* Coloss. i. 26 ff. ; Eph. iii. 9 ff ; ii. 12–20). Yet he seems to have dwelt upon it so convincingly and to have pressed it home so urgently that it became the possession of every despised Gentile within the Christian community. Let us try to realise what it must have meant for St Paul's converts to hear a sentence like this : " For as many of you as were baptized into Christ put on Christ. There is neither Jew nor Greek, there is neither slave nor freed man, there is neither male nor female : for you are all one man in Christ Jesus " (Gal. iii. 27, 28). Here is not only a mental, but also a social

B

revolution. All the supreme values of the
time are turned upside down. The liberating
truth of Jesus has obliterated the age-long
distinctions, making all the important things
new. What immense tasks the transformation
involved for the young society, tasks which even
up till now have been only feebly grappled with.

We can imagine that nothing so completely
startled the old world as this transforming
principle. It must have slowly recreated
thought, not merely custom or intercourse.
And yet I cannot believe that it was unknown
to any Christian of average intelligence in
St Paul's closing days. One is sure that many
good Jewish Christians shut their eyes to it
as long as they were able. For it seemed to
give the lie to all that they had held sacred.
The books of the New Testament bear witness
to the sharpness of the struggle between those
who accepted Paul's position and those who
did not.

But marvellous results followed from under-
standing what he meant. At one stroke,
wistful Gentiles who could only find scattered
rays of light in their own highly-prized literature, were able to serve themselves heirs to the
Old Testament. This was the most genuine
treasure-house upon which they had ever lit. It
appeared to supply them with all sorts of riches.
It gave them great religious ideas on which to
brood. It expressed their own unspoken and
unclarified thoughts and desires. It provided

them with a remarkable vocabulary in which to embody their religious experiences. The more curious minds were bound to busy themselves in adjusting the old revelation to the new, and in finding there notable foreshadowings of the things to come. Must we not admit that the central standpoint of every convert from Paganism might express itself in such forms as these : " I belong to the people of God, the chosen community of the Messiah ? " (*Cf.* 1 Peter ii. 1–10).

We can see, therefore, how there arose the remarkable conception of the Third Race (τρίτον γένος). This description appears first in literature towards the end of the second century, but it may quite well have originated at an earlier date. Its significance is far-reaching. It indicates that the Christian society had become well-known, for this was the fashion in which it was distinguished first, from Romans, and second, from Jews. It also suggests what is self-evident in the passages where it appears that the Christians formed an isolated group of people, characterised by certain peculiar features. I shall do no more than refer to the peculiarities assigned to them— their lack of images in worship which accounted for the charges of atheism brought against them, and their exclusiveness (ἀμιξία) which especially irritated their neighbours and gained for them all manner of abuse and the reckless imputation of shameful accusations (see especially Harnack, *Mission and Expansion of Christianity*, Eng. Tr., vol. i. pp. 266–278).

Let us attempt to picture one of those communities, say, in a town of the Diaspora, in Asia Minor by preference. Its nucleus would almost certainly be a little group of devout Jews, who had been persuaded by Paul or Barnabas or whatever Christian missionary had appealed to them, that Jesus of Nazareth was the Messiah. For some time they would scarcely recognise whether they had broken with the Synagogue or not. For in the Old Testament lessons read there and commented on they would discern with growing clearness the development which pointed to Christ. Round them would gather a circle of God-fearers (σεβόμενοι τὸν θεόν): men and women of Gentile origin, Greeks, Romans, Orientals, Aborigines, who had long craved for more spiritual force than that which their ancestral religions provided : people whose moral consciousness had never been satisfied. It was new life for them to hear of a transcendent, perfectly moral God, whose providential government of the world was entirely moral also : of One who, while spiritually holy, was willing to come into real spiritual contact with men : of One, whose character involved ethical issues for human life. This was also an eternal God, whose worshippers were assured of immortality. They had never become Jews, although they had prepared to occupy the devout Jewish

standpoint. But, as in the case of some of
their fellow-worshippers in the Synagogue,
their hearts had been touched more profoundly
by the Christian message. Like them they had
been led to discern in Christ the way to the
living God. So all alike had placed themselves
under Christian instruction. They had learned
the outlines of the life of Jesus, and the sum and
substance of His teaching. Their favourite Old
Testament had never been discarded : it rather
revealed to them with a new illumination the
unity of God's purpose all through the various
ages. Soon they were ready for the great
initial sacrament of Baptism, which was their
public testimony that they were facing a new
kind of existence : that for them old things
had passed away. This solemn rite entailed
various important consequences. In a real
sense it cut them off from their earlier environment and committed them to the fortunes of the
Christian society. No doubt they approached
it with serious anticipations. No doubt the
large majority of them, realising that they
were making their most momentous decision
and thus having all their spiritual energies
stirred, became conscious in their baptismal
experience of the moving of fresh moral forces
within them, of an increased nearness to the
presence of God, a more immediate grasp of
the life-giving energies of the exalted Christ.
In the case of many it would take long before
the impetus to patient moral activity along

the lines of Christ's own example was exhausted.
But the very rationale of the community aimed
at the opposite consequence. The men and
women who had come to share these wonderful
experiences were thrown into mutual intercourse. They would see much of each other,
and strengthen their common faith by dwelling
in conversation on its grounds of assurance.
They would strive to exemplify in this daily
intercourse the spirit and temper of Jesus, in
whom they had truly found God. Above all
else, their deeper fellowship would be brought to
light in the regular celebration of the Eucharist,
and the love-feasts with which it was associated.
The Eucharist, indeed, was intended to do far
more for them than express their spiritual one-
ness in Christ Jesus, although that itself was much.
It was meant to remind them of their individual and community relation to Christ. The
faith in Him which had led them to Baptism
was not something vague and undefined. At
its centre, no doubt, it defied explanation :
it was the union of the soul with its Lord, which
no one could analyse. But the individual was
meant to reflect on his devotion to the living
Lord. It was not an indistinct figure of a
Divine being to which he had pledged himself.
It was to Jesus as sacrificing His own life out
of sheer love for men, in circumstances of shame
and dishonour ; to Jesus who could not be
holden of death but had assured His followers
that He was alive for evermore and had the

Keys of Hades and of death; to Jesus who
had fulfilled what He promised by endowing
His disciples with unheard-of spiritual power.
The entire content of Christianity, it may
almost be said, was symbolised in this simple
meal, which was the pledging of themselves to
be loyal to Him who had spared nothing on
their account.

Plainly, such a community must have been
very informal. We must strip our minds of
all notions of sacred buildings and careful
organisation. Yet no corporate life can be
lived apart from certain arrangements and
regulations which are acknowledged by all.
The men of widest religious experience and
greatest organising skill would inevitably be
consulted as soon as a community had begun
to take shape. It could never indeed be
entirely helpless, for similar groups were to be
found all over the Roman Empire. And the
means of communication between widely-
separated regions were far more convenient
than we often imagine. Besides, intelligent
citizens had various models to follow. Much
light has, within recent years, been thrown upon
the busy guild-life which could be seen in every
important centre, more especially in the towns
which carried on an overseas trade. These
various guilds had their officials, who presided
at meetings, directed plans for the common
life, took charge of the money offered by
members for common purposes. Even for

Jews, who had no dealings with Greek guilds
or associations, there was the model of the
Synagogue. It had no rigid constitution,[1] yet
its arrangements were never allowed to fall
into chaos. It possessed "rulers," not necessarily men of special training, who took the
oversight of its affairs. This very flexibility
was a source of advantage in a time of transition, and with an indifferent or hostile environment. Suffice it to say that "elders"
(πρεσβύτεροι) were fundamental in the life of
the early Christian society.

But the key-note of Christian living was
service, in accordance with the Master's saying, "I am among you as he that serveth"
(Luke xxii. 27). And thus there soon came to
be formed a group of men and women called
"deacons" and "deaconesses" (Rom. xvi. 1;
Phil. i. 1; 1 Tim. iii. 8 ff) who must have found
multifarious duties lying to their hands. This
is not the place to discuss the more minute
and contested details of Church organisation,
but obviously, at an early date, certain of the
"elders" seem to have been selected for important functions, perhaps largely financial,
perhaps specially associated with the due
celebration of the Eucharist. These "over-
seers" (ἐπίσκοποι) were apparently the
original germ of the far-reaching *episcopal*
organisation, so fraught with significance for
later developments of the history of the Church.

[1] See Note I., *Religiones Licitæ*, p. 31.

This favourite term of ours, "Church," is both true to the facts and gravely misleading. A community of men and women who were "baptised into" Christ, who thereby professed their whole-hearted allegiance to Him, naturally became, in the circumstances of the time, exclusive. This new allegiance overshadowed everything else in their history. And as the days went on, its consequences, for most of them, stood out more important than ever. Whether they fully grasped what St Paul meant when he affirmed: "You are all one man in Christ Jesus" (Gal. iii. 28), one would not venture to say. But all the more reflective among them would realise the vast change that had taken place. Men and women, masters and slaves, Jew and Greek had sat down at the same Holy Table. They had joined on a common footing in the same simple worship. It is highly probable that frequently the chief officials of the community belonged to the servile class. Certainly slaves formed a large proportion of the membership of the society, as we know from early Christian literature, and as we find hinted at in prominent passages of the New Testament (e.g. 1 Cor. vii. 20–24; Coloss. iii. 22–25; Philemon, *passim*; 1 Peter ii. 18–25). They would soon feel that this community[1] stood by itself: that its guiding principles were wholly different from those of ordinary society. More especially, as its tone

[1] See Note II., *Ecclesia*, p. 32.

was very lax, and its aims thoroughly secular, that society would have no keen attraction for people who were over-awed by this new conception of God, and, at the same time, profoundly grateful for His generosity to them in Christ Jesus their Lord. Hence they did find much more pleasure and profit in their united gatherings within the community than anywhere else. Not that in the early days they had sacred or stately buildings to meet in. Most probably their earliest meeting-places were rooms in the houses of some of their more prosperous members, lent for the purpose and more or less prepared for worship. But the thought of the building suggests important aspects of the situation as a whole. The communities could not present the appearance of large congregations. It is hard to suppose that more than forty or fifty at the most could have met on single occasions of worship. It must not indeed be forgotten that sometimes open-air spaces would be at their disposal. And there is abundant evidence to show that at Rome they used the famous underground cemeteries of the Catacombs for their solemn gatherings, although we must not completely dissociate the fact from their existence under the guise of burial clubs.

Accordingly, their public life would rather take the shape of conventicles than anything else, and so might give the impression of purely private and mysterious associations. We know that that impression prevailed. But its force would be diminished by the acquaintance of the public with mystery-cults and associations, which were based on private initiations, and tended to emphasise both the spirituality of the Deity and the certainty of a blessed life to come for all the " redeemed." The supreme peril for societies of this kind is the bitter self-assertion of their more energetic members. There could be no higher testimony to the pervasion of the early communities with the Spirit of their Lord than their continuous existence and growth, which were not seriously disturbed until the flourishing period of Gnosticism in the second century.

We are largely ignorant as to the nature of the regular worship of the Church in the early days. We only state the facts that are undoubted. Probably they met several times in the week, but their most important gathering was held on Sunday. " On the so-called day of the Sun," says Justin the Martyr, writing towards the middle of the second century, " there is a meeting of all of us who live in cities or the country, and the memoirs of the Apostles or the writings of the prophets are read, as long as time allows. Then when the reader has ceased, the president gives by word of mouth his admonition and exhortation to follow these excellent things. Afterwards we all rise at once and offer prayers ; and as I said, when we have ceased to pray, bread is brought and wine and a cup of water, and the president likewise offers up prayers and thanksgivings to the best of his power, and the people assents with its Amen. Then follows the distribution to each and the partaking of that for which thanks was given; and to those that are absent a portion is sent by the hand of the deacons. Of those that are well-to-do and willing, every one gives what he will according to his own purpose, and the collection is deposited with the president, and he it is that succours orphans and widows, and those that are in want through sickness or any other cause, and those that are in bonds, and the strangers that are sojourning, and in short he has the charge of all that are in need" (*Apology*, i. 67). This statement is confirmed by some sentences in a letter from Pliny, the Roman proconsul, written about A.D. 112 to the Emperor Trajan, whose official he was. "The amount of their [*i.e.* the Christians'] fault or error was this that it was their habit on a fixed day to assemble before daylight and sing by turns a hymn to Christ as a god; and that they bound themselves with an oath, not for any crime [as had been alleged], but not to commit theft or robbery or adultery, not to break their word, and not to deny a deposit when demanded. After this was done, their custom was to depart, and meet together again to take food, but ordinary and harmless food; and even this (they said) they had given up doing after the issue of my edict,

by which in accordance with your commands
I had forbidden the existence of clubs " (*Epist.*
x. 96).

One or two remarks may be made. The
Christian meeting, as described by Justin, a
convert from Paganism, reminds us closely of
the Synagogue service. The reading of sacred
lessons is central for both passages. But we
note that the Memoirs of the Apostles are
included, while the Law of Moses is left out.
The life and teaching of Jesus have become the
New Law, the norm, in so far as there is a
norm, for Christian living. The words read
form, as in the Synagogue, the basis for a
direct religious exhortation to the people.
Prayer and praise (so Pliny) are mingled with
the service. Justin lays great emphasis on the
celebration of the Eucharist, in which absent
members are permitted to share, and upon the
offertory, which was evidently used to supply
the wants of individuals. Additional illumination is found in Tertullian's account of Christian
worship, an account altogether in line with
Justin's, but bringing into special prominence
the disciplinary function of the society. " We
are made a body," he says, " by common
religious feeling, unity of discipline, and the
bond of hope. We come together in a meeting
and assembly that we may as it were form a
troop, and so in prayer to God beset Him with
our supplications." After reminding them of
the high value of reading together " the divine

writings," and of the censorship exercised upon
sinners, Tertullian proceeds : " Even if there
is a sort of common fund, it is not made up of
money paid in fees, as for a worship by contract.
Each of us puts in a trifle on the monthly day,
or when he pleases ; but only if he pleases,
and only if he is able, for no man is obliged, but
contributes of his own free will.   These are as
it were deposits of piety ; for it is not paid out
thence for feasts and drinkings and thankless
eating-houses, but for feeding and burying the
needy, for boys and girls deprived of means
and parents, for old folk now confined to the
house : also for them that are shipwrecked, for
any who are in the mines, and for any who in
the islands or in the prisons, if only it be for
the cause of God's people, become the nurslings
of their own confession " (*Apologet.* 39).

What seems to have made the deepest impression on Tertullian was the liberality of the
community, or rather the altruistic use made
of all their contributions.   The relief of need
became an indissoluble part of public worship.
A new direction was given to their thoughts.
Uninfluential themselves, their chief concern
was to help those in circumstances of distress.
That   disposition   remained   typical   of   the
Christian Church.   It was a permanent contribution to the civilising and socialising of
the outside world.

Note I

Religiones Licitæ

We have noted that Christianity left the
impression on outside observers of being a new
sect of Judaism. This was not unnatural, as
there were so many points of agreement between them. Both were strong supporters
of monotheism. Both, in the early period,
engaged in a worship of God which was totally
devoid of idols. Both set apart one day in
the week for drawing near to the Deity, and
strove to make it as far as possible a day of
rest. Both were believers in a future life, in
which moral retribution was assigned a prominent place. Both laid great stress on the
"anointed" of God, the Messiah, Who was
equipped with Divine powers, Who possessed
the function of judging the world, and Whose
Kingdom was the goal of expectation. Both
insisted on the closest association of conduct
with religious profession.

But the most remarkable divergence between
them in the early Empire lay in the fact that
Judaism was recognised as a "religio licita," a
lawful religion, while Christianity was not.
This completely changed the attitude of the
authorities towards the respective faiths. The
Jews had reached their favoured position largely
through the influence of friends at court, and
by the payment of a tax imposed by Vespasian
after the destruction of Jerusalem, consisting

in the half-shekel originally paid for the upkeep of the Temple. Moreover, their propaganda was more tactful than that of the Christians. But even Judaism could by no means satisfy, *e.g.* Cicero's definition of "legal"—"that which is allowed by the laws and by the custom and institution of our ancestors " (Phil. xiii. 6, 14). Christianity was not only a " non-recognised religion," (*religio illicita*): it was condemned as a "factio," a " dangerous sect," under the Edict of Trajan, which forbade the formation of *collegia fabrum,* "associations of artificers," or *hetæriæ,* religious brotherhoods. See Plin. Epp. x. 39, 40, 96. [This evidence condensed from Mr Bindley's valuable notes on Tertullian's *Apologeticus,* iv. 12, xviii. 6, xxxviii. 1.]

It has, of course, to be noted that the Jews, as being a nation, were considered to have the right to adhere to the religious usages handed down by their fathers. The Christians, drawn from all peoples, ignored their historical past. This disloyalty to their ancestral customs was a main cause of the prejudice stirred up against them in the minds of otherwise clement emperors and subordinate officials, as well as in those of Roman citizens as a whole.

Note II

Ecclesia

We are aware from the usage of Acts (*e.g.* v. 11, viii. 1, ix. 31, etc.), that the first community of Christians at Jerusalem and then the extension of that community in different regions were called "ecclesiæ" (ἐκκλησίαι). The word and the idea have their origin in the Old Testament. The word was used by the translators of the Old Testament into Greek, from Deuteronomy onwards, as the rendering of Hebrew *qāhāl*, the "congregation" of Israel as assembled. Apparently, after the Exile, the latter term came to combine in itself the favourite expression in the Pentateuch, *'ēdhāh* (usually translated by συναγωγή in the LXX.) meaning strictly the "congregation" of Israel, along with its own peculiar significance of "assembly." Hence, as Hort says, ἐκκλησία "would naturally for Greek-speaking Jews mean the congregation of Israel quite as much as an assembly of the congregation" (*The Christian Ecclesia*, p. 7). The influence of this usage must have spread. Thus the late Psalm lxxiv. 2, "Remember thy congregation which thou didst purchase of old," where *ēdhāh* is the word for congregation, is used freely by St Paul in his address to the elders at Ephesus (Acts xx. 28), and there he deliberately employs ἐκκλησία instead of the Septuagint rendering, συναγωγή. "Fresh significance is given to the Psalmist's language by the way in which St Paul appropriates it to describe how God had purchased to Himself a new congregation (now called ἐκκλησία)" (Hort, *op. cit.* p. 14). These two Hebrew words,

c

whose history and usage are so closely inter-
twined, suggest "no mere agglomeration of
men, but rather a unity carried out in the joint
action of many members, each having his own
responsibility, the action of each and all being
regulated by a supreme law or order" (Hort,
op. cit. p. 15). Naturally, it is of primary
importance that it was on Jewish and not Greek
soil that the Christian Ecclesia was to take
shape. I do not discuss our Lord's use of the
term ἐκκλησία in Matt. xvi. 18, although I feel
that there is nothing there to suggest a second-
century interpolation, and agree with Hort that
"the most obvious interpretation" of His
famous words about Peter "is the true one"
(*op. cit.* p. 16).

The Epistles show how firm a place the
conception of the Ecclesia has taken in St Paul's
mind. From that time onwards the Ecclesia
involves a more or less recognised organisation.
It is practically equivalent to the Body of
Christ. But we must, of course, be on our
guard against identifying it in the early period
with our current conception of "Church." It
carries with it its Jewish associations, and for
long remains flexible in character. One of its
most important variations of meaning is that
from the local to the world-wide community.

QUESTIONS FOR DISCUSSION.

1. Why were some Christians opposed to the equalising of
   Jews and pagans ?

2. What did Baptism and Eucharist mean to the Early Church ?
3. How did the organisation of the Church begin ?
4. What was the relation of the Church to other associations and to the State ?
5. What were the most important elements in early Christian Services ?

For Further Reading.

The Book of the Acts. By Vernon Bartlet.

Article on "Paul," by G. G. Findlay, in *H.D.B.*

Christian Life in the Primitive Church, pp. 138-159. Dobschütz.

CHAPTER III

FRATERNITY

Col. iii. ; Eph. iv., v., vi. ; 2 Cor. ix. ; 1 Cor. xii., xiii.

I HAVE not yet singled out a most arresting feature of the early Christian community— that its various relationships were invariably described by St Paul as being " in the Lord." It is needless to quote passages. Every epistle rings with the idea. But if the Lord be thus the standard for all their mutual intercourse, that intercourse must receive a certain definite stamp. It becomes far more personal and intimate than it would otherwise be. It assumes the character of *brotherhood*. The deep foundation for this position is disclosed by the Epistles of St Paul. It is shown to be bound up with their religious attitude. It does not consist, that is to say, of mere clannishness and the obligations which spring from that. It goes back to their relationship towards God. It is as Father that God has called them into His Kingdom. Primarily, they have deliberately entered upon the relationship of children. They have become members of the same family, brothers in Christ Jesus. The mood and spirit of genuine brotherhood signalises the community from its very beginning.

The early chapters of Acts describe the
outcome of this temper. " Now all who
believed," says the writer, " kept together and
possessed all things in common, and they were
wont to sell their property and their goods,
and to distribute the proceeds among the rest,
according to the need of individuals ; and
daily they waited upon God together in the
Temple, and breaking bread in their several
houses they partook of their food with gladness
and simplicity of heart, praising God and
finding favour with all the people " (ii. 44–47).
And again : " One heart and one spirit prevailed among the multitude of believers, and
no one claimed any part of his property as his
own, but all belonged to them in common.
And with mighty power did the Apostles
testify to the resurrection of the Lord Jesus,
and great grace was upon them all. For no
one was in want among them, as all who
possessed lands or houses sold them and brought
the price from the sale and laid it at the
Apostles' feet. It was then distributed according to the individual's need " (iv. 32–35). This
is not the place to attempt an estimate of the
apparent communism, which was evidently
quite spontaneous and not the consequence of
theorising. Obviously it sprang from the type
of generosity which had a profound motive
behind it. Those Christian believers had no
plans in their minds. They were too dazed by
the marvellous new environment into which

they had passed to contemplate fixed arrangements. They were rather "as men that dreamed." The unfathomable generosity of Christ seemed to lay infinite obligations upon them. Nothing was too good for His service. Probably actions which involved self-sacrifice could alone satisfy their feelings.

But this was no mere unbalanced enthusiasm. Throughout years of patient obedience the spirit of unselfishness endured. At least as far down as Tertullian, writing at the opening of the third century A.D., the only limit recognised in the community was the *need* of individuals. The charity of the Early Christians, of which we have had various examples, covered a wide range. It began at home, attending to the claims of the church services, and caring for the support of those who gradually became official ministers of the community. A special charge was the support of widows and orphans who even in Pagan society appealed to the generosity of their neighbours. Both the New Testament and the writings of the Apostolic Fathers bear frequent testimony to this. But the sick, the maimed, the weak, the poverty-stricken, were never neglected. Thus it is prescribed for deacons in the Apostolic Constitutions (*T.U.* ii. 5, 8 f.): "They are to be doers of good works, exercising a general supervision day and night . . . they must ascertain who are in distress, and not exclude them from a share in

the Church funds, compelling also the well-
to-do to lay aside money for good works"
(Harnack, *op. cit.* E. Tr. I. p. 161). The kindness
of Christians extended to prisoners and those
condemned to work in the mines, a sphere of
beneficence which often led them into serious
dangers.

The large question of the treatment of
slaves belongs to the heart of our subject. At
no point was the new faith more severely
tested. For as yet the question had not
become a matter of public discussion. Such
a passage as 1 Cor. vii. 20 ff., indicates that for
a Christian leader like St Paul slavery was no
grievance. And it is most significant that in
his dealings with the Colossian Christian
Philemon about his slave Onesimus, he makes
no suggestion concerning the slave's liberation.
Yet the great principles of the faith, already
noted, secured a new outlook for these down-
trodden beings. " Slaves, male and female,"
says Aristides, early in the second century,
" are instructed so that they become Christians,
on account of the love felt for them by their
masters ; and when this takes place, they call
them brethren without any distinction whatever " (qd. by Harnack, *op. cit.* p. 168, n. 1).
The obliterating of all distinctions in Jesus
Christ began to tell from the very outset. It
is remarkable that two of the most famous
officials in the early Church at Rome, Pius, the
brother of Hermas, and Callistus, had originally

been slaves. Curiously enough, the title "slave" never occurs in the sepulchral inscriptions of the Christian community at Rome.

The presence of calamity of any kind was sufficient to call forth the charitable activities of Christians. Pontianus, the biographer of the famous African bishop Cyprian (close of second century, A.D.), gives an example of how he trained the people of his diocese in time of plague. "The people being assembled together, he first of all urges on them the benefits of mercy. By means of examples drawn from the sacred lessons he teaches them . . . then he proceeds to add that there is nothing remarkable in cherishing merely our own people with the due attentions of love, but that one might become perfect who should do something more than heathen men or publicans, one who, overcoming evil with good, and practising a merciful kindness like to that of God, should love his enemies as well. . . . What should a Christian people do, a people whose very name was derived from faith? The contributions are always distributed then according to the degree of the men, and of their respective ranks. Many who, on the score of poverty, could not make any show of wealth, display far more than wealth, as they made up by personal labour an offering dearer than all the riches in the world. Thus the good done was done to all men, and not merely

to the household of faith, so richly did the
good works overflow " (Harnack, *op. cit.*
p. 172 f.). Here is a noteworthy feature. The
loving interest of the community extends far
beyond its own borders. An opportunity is
given to Pagans of testing its sincerity. Who
can doubt that over and over again the true
impression was gained ?

It is plain from the evidence which has
been adduced that the members of the community had penetrated to the core of their
religion. The habit of caring intensely for
the needs of others had been learnt from Jesus,
and it accorded completely with His main
lesson—that God is Love. It carried into
effect the fundamental views of St Paul and
the Fourth Gospel. The watchword of the
early community was that which the First
Epistle of John set in the forefront : " We
love because He first loved us " (1 John iv. 19).
To go back upon that was to be disloyal to the
central message of the Gospel.

But how could this motive operate ? How
did it succeed in giving the characteristic tone
to the variegated Christian community ? If we
are to be true to the data, we must acknowledge the amazing sense of power of which the
Apostles speak again and again, and of which
St Paul is the most famous witness. There
can be no question that it was he who gave
the community the proper consciousness of
what it possessed. It is plain from many

passages in Acts that early believers were struck by the abnormal phenomena which appeared in the life of the Church. They were disposed to associate these with the ordinance of Baptism, which assumed a growingly mystical character as those who belonged to Greek and Oriental religious associations flocked into the society. The parallel between the solemn, though simple, rite, and the esoteric, semi-magical ritual of the mysteries was bound to impress their minds, and to react on their beliefs. Often they connected the phenomena with the laying on of hands, a ceremony which seemed to invite the idea of the conveyance of some unearthly grace. St Paul, in his wisdom, quickly discerned the superficial interpretations which would be reached. But he also became alive to the waste of spiritual energy involved in such practices as " speaking with tongues." [1] He fully recognised the extraordinary value set upon them. What made the situation more difficult, he did not feel at liberty to disown them. He believed that some strange Divine influence was involved in them. But he has no hesitation in declaring that the sole criterion to be applied to the endowment is its power of benefitting the brethren (1 Cor. xiv. 12, 19, 26, 40). There are other manifestations of the Divine Spirit of Power, to be esteemed far more highly. The best gift of all is abounding love. One can scarcely doubt

[1] See Note III., on *Speaking with Tongues*, p. 45.

that it was the life and practice of Jesus which
was before St Paul's mind when he dictated
his famous hymn of love (1 Cor. 13).

But the discussion which culminates in that
celebrated chapter is of immense importance
for disclosing the roots of the Apostle's thought.
The community, he recognises, is characterised
by all sorts of temperaments, and all sorts of
possibilities. The last thing to be aimed at
is uniformity. The secret of the Society's
strength is the manifoldness of its powers. To
them correspond the spiritual functions which
it is in a position to discharge. St Paul had
become acquainted with these facts as a
practical missionary and church-builder. He
penetrates their significance as a daring
architect of the spiritual life. He will not
shrink from a bold metaphor. "As the
Body is one and yet has many members ($\mu\acute{\epsilon}\lambda\eta$ =
limbs), but all the members of the Body although
numerous constitute one body, so also is
Christ" (1 Cor. xii. 12).

It is needless to investigate, as some have
done, the origin of this metaphor. As in
most cases, it is improbable that that should
be traced to a single source. Plainly, the conception of the one spirit would be bound to
suggest that of one body, more especially as
its function was so widely conceived to be
unifying. But it would also be prompted by
the idea of diversity which would certainly force
itself on men's attention. Here is a widely-

scattered group, made up of every type. Its antecedents, as regards birth, training, position and environment, are endlessly varying. It is held together by its common attitude of faith in Jesus Christ, in the profoundest sense of the term. That involves not only activity of will but also receptivity. Now this latter means especially openness to the Divine influence. The form in which the writers of the period clothe the notion of the Divine gift is the Holy Spirit. The Spirit of God reinforces the innate capacities of men and women, fitting each for the special service which he or she is able to render. And the proper realisation of brotherhood is the placing of these capacities at the Divine disposal. Each function performed is nothing less than a testimony to the goodness of God in Christ. " She hath done what she could "—that was Jesus' own defence of the conduct of a woman which was censured even by His followers.

Accordingly, the realisation of brotherhood is not a sphere tacked on to ordinary life. It is that life viewed in its highest power ; revealing its real spiritual value for the good of others. It is trained within the narrower community in order that it may expand, and claim the whole world for the ideal of Christ.

NOTE III

Speaking with Tongues

One of the most remarkable features of the First Epistle to the Corinthians is the references made by St Paul to that spiritual endowment which is described in the New Testament as " speaking with tongues " We remember the prominent place in the Christian life which he assigns to the operation of the Holy Spirit. It may almost be said that one of the tests for a Christian is his possession of some spiritual " gift " ($\chi\acute{\alpha}\rho\iota\sigma\mu\alpha$). For equipment with the Spirit ought normally to impart to the individual some capacity which will minister to the good of the community to which he belongs, as a whole. The very existence of the community is held together by the bonds of mutual service. Such service is composed of a great variety of functions, each of which has its proper place in the relation of its members to the Body of Christ. The Apostle discusses the diverse functions at considerable length in 1 Cor. xii, but it is plain from the discussion that one particular gift overshadows all others at Corinth. The chief ambition of the members of that community is to be able to speak with tongues ($\gamma\lambda\acute{\omega}\sigma\sigma\alpha\iota\varsigma$ $\lambda\alpha\lambda\epsilon\hat{\iota}\nu$). What did the gift mean ?

We are here confronted by one of those remarkable phenomena which are visible all the world over in times of religious ferment. The

external manifestation consists in the bursting
into ejaculations usually of praise and prayer
of men and women who seem to be possessed
by a force outside their own personalities
which defies their control. Sometimes the
utterances are less excited, more regulated and
continuous. Often the condition gradually
pervades a large section of the gathering, as it
were by physical contagion. The sounds made
are constantly of a character which gives the
impression to most of the audience of some
strange language they have never learnt. But
curiously enough, some members of the
audience may profess to understand the utterances, and may interpret them to the rest of
the listeners. This capacity, whether real or
imagined, seems also to have been regarded as
a " gift " by the early Christian communities.

St Paul, with his practical insight, sets
himself to pronounce his estimate of the various
spiritual endowments. Plainly, he is some-
what perplexed by this particular phenomenon.
He does not hesitate to acknowledge it as a
gift of the Spirit. But while refraining from
words of censure, he is quite ready to put it
in its proper place. He will not assign it a
high rank, because it has no necessary bearing
on the edification of the community. He
regards its exercise as a matter between God
and the soul of the Christian. It is a waste of
spiritual energy, unless there be some one
present who can interpret. And he fears the

effect of witnessing it upon outside enquirers
who may easily form the impression that the
speaker is drunk. He greatly prefers allied
gifts, such as that which he calls " prophesying."
That, also, is the result of the Spirit's working,
but it means the proclamation to the community
of profound spiritual truths, which can only
be discerned by Divine help, but which can
illuminate religious or moral problems for the
minds of the hearers. This, as being speech
accompanied by mind ($\nu o \hat{\upsilon} \varsigma$), he sets high
above those more mysterious utterances which
seem to be devoid of rationality, entirely
compacted of heightened religious emotion.

QUESTIONS FOR DISCUSSION.

1. What is the secret of Christian brotherhood ?
2. What is the significance of the metaphor of the " body "
    as applied to the Church ?
3. What did the early Christians mean by the Holy Spirit ?

FOR FURTHER READING.

The Holy Spirit in Faith and Experience, pp. 205–251.   By
    A. L. Humphries.

CHAPTER IV

LIBERTY

Acts xv. ; Gal. ii. ; Rom. xiv., xv. ; Mark vii. 1-23 ; Acts x.

To pretend that the life of the Early Church was uninterrupted progress would be to falsify the facts, even as these appear on the pages of writers who were prepared to view them in the most favourable light. Stubborn, self-willed human nature cannot be transformed even in a generation. The birth of Christianity belonged to a period of fundamental transition. The East had begun to flow into the West. And in the East itself revolution had followed the campaigns of Alexander the Great and the wars of his successors. A process of unification had set in. But experience teaches how tardy such processes are apt to be, and how long they remain external. There must have been a gradual breaking-down of barriers between Jew and Gentile in the Diaspora.[1] But the actual preparation for such advances is usually painful and provokes grievous misunderstandings. The more rough-and-ready temperaments are irritated. Those of conservative taste are alarmed. The pioneers are urged on by impetuosity.

[1] See Note IV., *The Diaspora*, p. 58.

The disciples of Jesus had made no plans for the steps in the development of the new community. The realisation of the Spirit may have prejudiced their minds against ordinary prosaic arrangements. There is almost a tone of impatience in the words of the Twelve, as reported in Acts vi. 3, 4. But that chapter itself shows how inevitably matters of business intrude into the most spiritual societies. Indeed, the early dispute is highly significant for the future. The Church was to all intents and purposes confined to Jerusalem, but already contentious subjects were seen to be involved in the relation of Palestinian Christians to Jewish disciples of the Diaspora. This tendency to estrangement between Palestinian and Diaspora Jews was one of those impalpable sentiments which does not admit of easy analysis. Of course, certain broad contrasts can be drawn. Men and women brought up in a Pagan environment were bound to be more open-minded than those trained in the atmosphere of Pharisaism. But generalisations would be rash. There must have been all kinds of divergences of feeling in the larger communities. This divergence would mainly depend on temperament and training. Of course, tradition would exercise a strong influence.

Now such differences probably existed among the inner circle of the Twelve, and the Christian leaders who stood nearest to them.

D

Inborn prejudices are the last strongholds of
the nature to yield even to the most spiritual
influences. Such prejudices and ancestral presuppositions had to submit to a hard test.

Fortunately we possess a large body of
evidence for the great crisis in the early history
of the Church in Acts xv. and Galatians ii.[1]
Confusion has been brought into the question
by those scholars who have imagined that the
events of Gal. ii. synchronise with those of
Acts xi. 27–30. To me, at least, it is clear that
St Paul, with breathless emotion, recounts in
Gal. ii. 1–10. that visit of Barnabas and himself
to Jerusalem, which is described in Acts xv.
as the result of the appearance of certain
zealous Jewish Christians from Jerusalem in
the Church of Antioch in Syria.

The story in Acts tells how, after their
return from their first missionary tour, Barnabas
and Paul [2] resumed their labours at Antioch.
Here they were working in a mixed community
of Jews, Greeks and Syrians. Their efforts
flourished until the arrival of the Jerusalem
Christians mentioned above, who "came in
stealthily," Paul boldly says (Gal. ii. 4), "to
spy out our freedom which we have in Christ
Jesus." Immediately there arose the controversy which was bound sooner or later to
come. The Christian missionaries were pro-
claiming their message to Jews and Greeks

---

[1] See Note V., *Acts and Galatians*, p. 60.
[2] See Note VI., *St Paul and St Luke*, p. 63.

indiscriminately. Apparently the conditions laid down for their reception into the Church made no distinction between them. Uncircumcised Pagans who had formerly been idolaters were admitted on the same terms as circumcised Jews, full members of the Old Testament community. The visitors were shocked at this laxity. They had evidently never realised that Christianity was far more than a mere subordinate sect of Judaism. In this respect they probably represented the view which prevailed at Jerusalem. To them it seemed nothing less than profane that former outcasts should, on profession of faith in Christ and the Baptism to which it led, succeed to the precious heritage of the chosen people, without being compelled to identify themselves with them. What was the object of that providential care which had preserved their fathers through so many vicissitudes untainted from the contaminations of a Pagan world ? Had the Divine energy been wasted in safeguarding them from a perilous environment ? Such objections would seem reasonable even to many right-thinking Jewish Christians.

The situation was serious. Probably St Paul alone grasped its full significance. He saw that a deliberate decision must be faced. That, of course, lay with the leaders at Jerusalem. Most scholars would agree that the narrative of Gal. ii. 1–10 gives the clearest and most correct view of the circumstances. These verses reveal that Paul demanded a private conference with the authorities, at which certain resolutions were fixed. There is no trace of any examination of principles. The main argument for freedom used by the missionaries from Antioch seems to have been the actual success of their work. This they could point to with pride. The same spiritual phenomena had been manifest in the case of Pagans as of Jews. There was no difference in earnestness or faithfulness. In either instance, it was plainly the Divine operation.

The Jerusalem authorities could not deny these data. And it is obvious that their consciences must have been troubled. The men of deeper spirituality like Peter and John must have begun to awake out of a sort of dream. The combination of events for which they had neglected to provide had occurred. The growth of the new community had been taken out of their hands. God was in the midst of it. Dare they fight against Him? The record in Galatians narrates that they came to a simple decision. They divided up the mission-field into two separate spheres, the Jewish and the Gentile. The former they placed under the superintendence of Peter, the latter under that of Paul. Their method of recognising in an elementary fashion the unity of the Christian movement consisted in a solemn invitation to Paul to interest Pagan communities in their Jewish-Christian brethren, by persuading them to help the poor of the Mother Church by contributions for their support.

Acts recounts a further step, which, to say the least, is shrouded in obscurity. Its narrative is concerned with a public meeting of Christians at Jerusalem, at which addresses were given by Paul, Barnabas, Peter, and James. The outcome of the deliberations is summed up in a message "to the Gentile brethren in Antioch and Syria and Cilicia" (xv. 24). It embodies the following resolution : "that Gentile Christians should abstain from sacrificial meat and blood and strangled flesh and fornication" (xv. 28, 29). Here is promulgated a regulation about food and impurity. We know how strict the Jews were on the subject of table-fellowship (*e.g.* Mark ii. 16 ff). This must have been closely associated with their codified laws concerning food (*e.g.* Lev. ii. ; Mark vii.). There was no point on which their relations with Gentiles was more rigidly guarded. Now in a mixed Christian community difficulties of this kind were sure to arise. The same thing would be true of impurity. The very rationale of the society was brotherhood. This relationship found expression in the central rite of the Church, the Lord's Supper. No distinction could be tolerated. All believers in Christ must sit down at the Holy Table on a common footing. But what would happen if such a meal were impossible ?

In Gal. ii. 11 ff. St Paul records how St Peter, perhaps the leading Christian in the Mother Church, paid a long visit to Antioch to examine the mission work for himself. He made himself the friend of all, and showed no scruples about sharing in common meals with Gentile converts until some bigoted members of the Church arrived from Jerusalem. He then identified himself with the rigid Jewish standpoint and renounced his former practice. The power of his influence was so marked that others who had occupied the broader position, like Barnabas, went back on their earlier procedure. Paul was so stirred by their inconsistency that he sternly rebuked Peter and his coadjutors in presence of the assembled community. He realised how deeply their action penetrated : how seriously it endangered the truth of his Gospel. He makes no mention of the Jerusalem resolution, forwarded to Gentile Christians in Antioch, Syria and Cilicia. If that had been decreed *before* Peter's visit to Antioch, he would only have required to refer to it. Taking a complete view of the circumstances, I am disposed to agree with those scholars who believe that the author of Acts ante-dated the so-called "Apostolic Decrees" : and that these were really due to the *contretemps* at Antioch. It seems highly probable that the "Decrees" were intended to meet just such a situation as Peter created, which must frequently have arisen on the mission-field. It is not surprising that a historian, writing many years after the events, should fall into confusion about some of the details.

In any case, these experiences enabled St Paul once for all to vindicate his position. He felt that he was confronted with a question of life and death. The whole future of Christianity was at stake. If he consented to the religion of Christ remaining a superior kind of Judaism, then he must revise all his fundamental ideas of it. If he were to be true to the most impressive elements in his own Christian experience, he must allow no tradition, however valuable in itself, to interfere with his interpretation of the facts.

Now it was the interpretation forced upon him which had changed his life. His conversion was no speculative process. It was a new view of God and the world which laid hold upon him through the medium of the living Christ. He had long wrestled with the *legal* type of religion embodied in Judaism. At every turn it clogged his zeal to go deeper. But when he, the bitter persecutor of the Nazarenes, met Jesus of Nazareth and became convinced that He was alive for evermore, almost all the categories which he had applied to God were changed. For, circumstantially, it was a new view of God which illuminated his soul. The God whom he met in the risen and living Jesus was above all else compassionate, the Lover of men.

That God should seek him out, the proud, bigoted Pharisee : that He should fill his soul with spiritual power ; that He should disclose to him something of the meaning of the love of Christ, seemed a miracle, a supernatural intervention. Although it was all the result of grace, it drove him to reflect upon himself. And he speedily discovered that now the method of legalism in religion was futile. A minute code of regulations regarding things to do, and things to avoid, appeared in the light of Christ's self-sacrifice, irrelevant. That could not be the path by which to approach God. Had it been, he would never have reached the position where he now stood. For as he came to examine himself, racial privileges and prerogatives fell away. He could claim nothing except on the ground of Christ's unfathomable love, which was not determined by a man's Judaism or his barbarism, but only by his infinite need.

Now this love, grasped by the soul, became a motive of marvellous effectiveness in the inner life. It always prompted to obedience. How could any man look it in the face without realising the obligations it laid upon him ? But it carried with it no trace of the old feeling of compulsion. The new relation to God disclosed in Christ was pre-eminently a relation of freedom. If God's supreme desire was the

Sonship of men, this was something voluntary, spontaneous, the glad movement of the soul. Now this was what the great apostle was concerned about. He is convinced that nothing is of value in religion which is forced. Men cannot be *taught* religion. The reality of the heart of God must flash upon them, and take possession of them. And this life of obedience must flow from that experience like a stream from its source. By all means let us learn to recognise the various phases in our spiritual training, however rudimentary they may have been, but let us insist on leaving the rudiments behind and entering into the fulness of our inheritance. That is open to us, not as a prize to be earned and to be awarded after a wearisome and miserable struggle. It is the gift of God now. It is free, and is intended for a free spirit.

So that the conflicts through which St Paul and others had to pass for the sake of what they called "the truth of the Gospel" became their instruments for setting forth what the Gospel really was. It is almost a truism that no disputed subject can be properly understood except as the result of argument. In that way alone can its less prominent issues take their proper place. Hence we may adapt the words of the Apostle, used in a totally different connection, and say that his struggles "turned out rather for the furtherance of the Gospel" (Phil. i. 12). Through them was disclosed its

essential character and its amazing possibilities.
The fifth chapter of Galatians is witness to the
rich variety of Paul's discoveries in this region.

NOTE IV

The Diaspora

The precise character of the Jewish people
in the Diaspora, *i.e.* of those scattered throughout the provinces and towns of the Roman
Empire, away from Palestine, presents a most
complex problem. We know that long before
the Christian era large settlements of Jews had
been established throughout that area. And
we would fain ascertain their attitude to their
environment, its habits and customs, its social
life, its philosophical movements, its religious
aspirations. Our evidence is very scanty.
Moreover, on that which we have it would be
unsafe to dogmatise. For there can scarcely
have been any common practice.

If, however, we reflect on the situation in
the light of the New Testament documents
which have been written by Jews of the Dispersion, we are, I think, bound to assume that
they breathed a freer air than their brethren
in Palestine. Yet even this would vary according to tradition and temperament. In the
case of some, sojourn in a foreign land would
accentuate the spirit of bigotry and create
aversion to the atmosphere around them in
all its elements. Those who kept in close

touch with Jerusalem, like St Paul's family, would probably be conscious of a proud isolation. But many must have formed friendships with Pagans, and their influence would have a silent though none the less powerful effect. Unquestionably the whole situation must have been affected by the relation of earnest Pagans towards the Synagogue. We know that those who had yielded to the craving for moral progress, characteristic of the time, were regular frequenters of Jewish worship. They valued the conception of the One God, pre-eminently a God of character, of a moral government of the world which pointed forward to retribution, of a future life which illuminated the darkness of the grave. These genuine enquirers must have, in their time, given the impulse to various modifications of the more rigid Jewish position. So we need not be surprised to find echoes of Hellenistic culture here and there in the Epistles. Indeed, the marvel is that many more do not occur. The only valid conclusion is that early Christianity made so supreme a demand upon its adherents, that they were mainly interested in its special counsels, its regular directions for life.

Still, the mission, through its Diaspora experiences, must have learnt invaluable lessons. The preachers, mostly Jews, must have came into close contact with Pagan enquirers. Mutual conversation would set in a fresh light many of the matters which caused perplexity to both. The Christian leaders would necessarily receive an insight into Pagan habits of religious thought which would equip them for their further work. No doubt the finest elements on both sides would be emphasised. It may, therefore, be said that the work of the Christian preachers must have been one of the most potent agencies in raising the whole standard both of religion and of civilisation throughout the Dispersion. And we can hardly doubt that there they had far more favourable access to the Jews than elsewhere. Of course we read of incidents which reveal racial narrowness, but Luke was not concerned to give *details* of those situations in which the message of new life and hope was received with welcome.

Note V

Acts and Galatians

Mention has already been made of the criteria which we must try to apply to those who wrote the New Testament books *as writers*. One of the chief points of application for such criteria is to be found in the relation of Galatians as written by St Paul to Acts as the work of St Luke. It is a simple matter to discuss this subject hastily and roughly. But we can only come within sight of the reality by self-control and careful handling. The main problem is the contrast between the

information which St Paul has supplied concerning his career *after* his conversion and
that compiled by St Luke regarding the same
period.

To begin with, we must always start with a
bias in favour of one who professes to describe
the experiences through which he passed as
against a writer who, long after the events,
has endeavoured to collect as many traditions
as he can, partly from the most trustworthy,
partly from less reliable sources. But that
consideration is by no means sufficient. We
have especially to discover, if we can, what
main purpose the respective authors had in
their minds when they set down the pictures
of the situation which they have left for us.

St Paul's aim in the relevant passages of
Galatians is to set forth as clearly as
possible his dependence in every step he took
on Jesus Christ and not on the original Apostles.
Hence he makes little of several important
events such as the visit he paid to Jerusalem
at the time when he had to leave Damascus
for fear of his life. All that he sets himself to
bring out is the brevity of his stay in Jerusalem,
the scantiness of his acquaintance with the
apostolic circle, and the unfamiliarity of the
Churches in Judea with himself. Luke, in
Acts, occupies a different standpoint. What
he emphasises in this Jerusalem visit is the
hesitation of the disciples there to have intimate
relations with the former persecutor. Barnabas

is the intermediary who makes himself the champion of Paul and really introduces him into the apostolic circle. In these favourable circumstances Paul is bold to confront the unbelieving Greek-speaking Jews, and becomes so notable because of his arguments with them that they plot against him. Whereupon the Christian brethren send him away to Tarsus.

It is quite easy to see how the same situation can be regarded from these differing points of view. And we do not require to estimate otherwise the famous visit of Paul and Barnabas paid from Antioch to Jerusalem. In Galatians (ii.) Paul dwells upon the all-important private conference in which the validity of his mission work was to be determined. He makes no reference to any public meeting at which addresses are given by prominent apostles. Probably he is thoroughly aware that the private conference reached the final decision, the frank recognition of his self-denying work. In Acts Luke completely passes over this preliminary gathering upon which everything depended, and lays the whole stress upon the public meeting, which consisted chiefly in the bearing of unhesitating testimonies to the value of Paul's labours among the Gentiles. It seems highly probable that both such assemblages were held. No doubt, the more private conference came to the authoritative decisions, and thus, as so frequently in the history of the Church, prepared the business for the public meeting

whose main function was the ratification of
these decisions. It may quite well be surmised
that Luke knew nothing of the earlier con-
sultation. To suppose that because Luke
appears to have been a direct witness of Paul's
fortunes in the second part of Acts, he must
therefore have been intimately acquainted with
the entire course of his life, is to misapprehend
the nature of ancient biographical writing.

What Luke was chiefly concerned to
guarantee, when he put together the Book of
Acts not long before the close of the first
century, was the ultimate agreement of the
leading Christian apostles on the fundamental
principles of the missionary enterprise. It
was a satisfaction for his mind to be able to
point to the brotherly harmony on the profoundest questions of honoured leaders who
had long since gone to their rest. The last
thing he will allow himself to do is to stir the
embers of dead controversies, or recall the strifes
which at one period had all but shattered the
early community.

NOTE VI

St Paul and St Luke

People are at last beginning to realise the
importance of New Testament Introduction;
to recognise that each paragraph and each
document in the New Testament is not to be

studied in isolation, but in the light of the occasions which prompted them and the environments from which they sprang. We must, therefore, be careful not to dogmatise too freely on the character, tone, and tendencies of any particular writer. It is easy and perhaps satisfying to affix labels to their names, but this is sure to be misleading. It is always difficult to put yourself back into the mind and motive of ancient writers.

The slightest consideration of the varying circumstances in which the two famous writers, St Paul and St Luke, took in hand the work of composition may well put us on our guard. Practically all the Pauline Epistles are called forth by pressing situations which the Apostle has to meet. He is under the constraint of the situation. He sets himself either to exhibit his attitude towards some particular danger or heresy without qualification, or he recalls events in the past which affect his present bearing without attempting to tone down the description which he seeks to make as impressive as possible. Thus, in trying to convince the Galatians of his complete independence of the original apostles, he almost leaves the impression that he never desired to learn anything of Jesus or of the early Christian position from the leaders in the Mother Church. But here we must discount his immediate aim. If he were considering the question from a different angle, he would not have hesitated to acknowledge his debt to those who were in Christianity before him.

St Luke occupies an entirely different position. He writes at a date at which the sharp Pauline controversies are past. He has no wish to accentuate the difficulties which had seemed so serious at an earlier time. These discords have been forgotten. It would be unfair to say that he draws a veil over the strifes. But a writer will inevitably group events in the main perspective which is clear to himself, and he will not insert details, even if they form part of his tradition, which might, in his judgment, distort the real movement of history.

QUESTIONS FOR DISCUSSION.

1. On what ground did the early Church open its doors to Gentile converts ?
2. What was the heart of the Gospel for St Paul ?

FOR FURTHER READING.

Critical Introduction to the New Testament, pp. 125–135.   By A. S. Peake.

CHAPTER V

Acts xxvi. ; Gal. i. ; 2 Cor. iv. ; Rom. v., viii. ; 1 Cor. xiii.

Our last chapter must have suggested the central importance for the early community of St Paul's personal discovery. The supreme moments in the history of the race have been associated with great human figures who have summed up in themselves the transforming tendencies of their times. We have only to think of names like Moses, David, Gautama, Zarathustra, Socrates, Mohammed, Luther, Knox, and others, to realise what I mean. Many obscure phases of their lives may remain veiled to us, but we discern in the man as a whole the epitome of forces striving to take shape in society. Human progress is a series of impulses. Each of these urges on the race to a point it has never before reached. Let us dwell for a little on the significance of the crisis in this man's life. St Paul had the rare privilege of belonging both to the Jewish and the Hellenic world. Born, as he tells us, in Tarsus, an important city of the Roman Empire, of a family which possessed the highly-coveted prerogative of Roman citizenship, but which, none the less, remained firmly loyal to

its Jewish origin, he would be exposed at an
early age to the influences of later Greek
culture. Tarsus was the seat of a famous
Stoic university, and at a time when thought
deliberately aimed at being popularised, this
must have meant much for the more talented
Jewish minds. Paul's outlook on life could
scarcely be as rigid as that of the ordinary
Palestinian Jew. But that need not mean
the lowering of religious standards. As a
fact, we know that he was in early youth sent
up to Jerusalem to receive a thorough training
at the hands of the Pharisees. We have little
light on these student days of his. It is useless
to discuss such questions as whether he had
ever seen or known Jesus. Nothing in his
Epistles seems to necessitate that, and he never
refers to the matter himself.

When we first see him, he is identified with
the extreme party in Judaism, those who from
the outset had been suspicious of the Nazarenes
and were now determined to root them out.
Paul was one of the abettors of Stephen's
martyrdom, and consistently with that position
he became a foremost persecutor of the Christian society. We should give much to know
the history of his inner life during this period.
As it is, we are obliged to form a kind of
imaginary portrait, based on certain passages
in his letters. These show that this determined leader, for all his ruthlessness, was
scarcely at ease in his convictions. He was

bending every effort to obey and defend the law, to justify his place among the more bigoted Pharisees, and yet his heart was not satisfied. He felt perilously uncertain of gaining God's favourable verdict, of being justified at the day of reckoning. His conscience was too sensitive to feel that his obedience was sufficient. And everything, of course, depended upon that.

When the living Jesus was revealed to him on the Damascus road, the first impression created in Paul's soul was the graciousness and gentleness of the Lord. There were no reproaches because of his past conduct, but an attitude of immeasurable love. But the crisis meant more than that. It was a paralysing shock to the young bigot's self-confidence. He had never ceased to denounce Jesus of Nazareth as an impostor. The crucifixion, a cursed death in the eyes of a Jew, put the stamp of blasphemy on His claim to be God's Messiah, the fulfiller of all the hopes of the nation. His death seemed to Paul the just penalty of all His delusive teaching. His alleged resurrection was merely the ruse of His deceived followers. To be convinced that Jesus *was* risen and alive for evermore worked a revolution in Paul's mind. This was an event unheard of, which at once suggested that He was unique. It accorded with all that He had forecasted. It really meant God's vindication of Jesus ; the proof that

the Divine life was in Him and with Him.
What the overpowered Pharisee had to do was
to interpret all that had happened in the light
of his discovery. We do not know how long
he took to reach satisfying positions regarding
the faith in Jesus the Messiah. But we can
discover how they affected his personal thinking. The death of Christ could not be a
disgrace. It must be a glory, in the Divine
purpose. It could only be grasped when the
believer recognised that sheer love lay behind
it, and that that was not intended to propitiate God, but was the love of God Himself.
Paul had to discover that the path of suffering
is alone the way into the Father's presence :
that membership of the human race implies
suffering : that true obedience is faithfulness
to God's will through suffering. He had to
realise that the clash between the holy Divine
purpose and defiled, selfish, human wills can
lead to no end but suffering and sorrow, which
involve the innocent at least as fully as the
guilty. Nothing but the Divine Love which
shone from the Cross was powerful enough
to humble the sinful soul before God, and to
reveal its entire dependence upon His generosity.
That, above all else, was St Paul's discovery
—that whatever satisfaction of soul comes to
a man, whatever free relationship towards
God he can assume, is not the result of painful
effort, but the recognition by a child of his
Father's heart. No Table of Commandments

had been of any avail.   To *know* God, as Jesus
had revealed Him, that was the secret of
triumphant life.

Here he found a home for the Christian
community.   This was what made him a
missionary to the Pagan world.   His gospel
belonged to a level where the old distinctions
between races, ranks, and creeds were necessarily ignored, he must chiefly appeal to man
as man, entreating his hearers to accept the
truth of his discovery.

It is difficult to say how far Paul was understood.   The phenomena of the second century
suggest that his message in many respects rose
above the heads of his hearers.   But the power
of the man could not be ignored.   For eyes
that could see, he had revealed marvellous
depths in the ways of God's working through
Jesus Christ.   He had laid the foundation for
subsequent religious thought, and even speculation.   His structure was continued by the
Fourth Gospel and those who were influenced
by it.   But he was not only a thinker : he
was also a great practical administrator.   He
established the methods of successful organisation.   No vigorous missionary could afford
to neglect the steps which St Paul was accustomed to take.   After the Gospels, which in-
corporated the principal traditions of the life
and teaching of Jesus, the Epistles of St. Paul
were collected into a *corpus*, which ranked only
second to those *memorabilia* of the early

disciples. His name and authority remained influential in the community. All the fresh apprehensions of the Divine grace and goodness in Jesus Christ reached subsequently in the history of the Church, owed their vitality to a renewed grasp of the Apostle's convictions. The recollection of his power of "becoming all things to all men" provided the chief norm of pastoral efficiency. The power of his impact upon other lives could never be ignored.

I have hinted that St. Paul's remarkable experience would probably fix a kind of criterion for entrance into the community but it would be dangerous to over-rate the influence of this. Then, as now, men must have identified themselves with Christianity along very different lines. Christ makes entirely divergent appeals to different men.[1] It is quite likely that from the first a definite type of conversion was the presupposition of candidates for baptism. From then until now discussion has never ceased regarding the *beginning* of the Christian life. But the teaching of experience warns us against trying to stereotype the process. To insist upon one kind of religious sensitiveness as indispensable to a genuine choice of the new life is to misconceive the method of God's working and the constitution of human nature. No doubt it was natural that on the mission field, in the case of multitudes, who had accepted without questioning the standard of

[1] See C. Moody, *The Heathen Heart*, passim.

morality prevailing around them, the transformation of life should be sudden and decisive. This, however, is far from settling the probabilities in other circumstances and other environments.

QUESTIONS FOR DISCUSSION.

1. What did the resurrection of Jesus mean to St Paul ?
2. What is meant by contrasting the Gospel with the Law ?
3. What is conversion ?

FOR FURTHER READING.

St Paul to the Romans. By R. L. Pelly.
Christian Freedom, pp. 137–184. By W. M. Macgregor.

CHAPTER VI

THE NEW AGE

2 Cor. v. ; Col. ii. ; 1 Cor. i., ii. ; 2 Cor. iii. ; 1 John iv.

ONE of the most famous of St. Paul's definitions of what a Christian is occurs in 2 Cor v. 17 : " If any one be in Christ, he is a new creature " (καινὴ κτίσις). The statement reflects his own case and that of many converts in the churches which he founded. Nothing more truly expresses what had happened than these daring words.

We have already tried to form some estimate of one aspect of the situation described in the passage quoted above. We have attempted to realise the new attitude towards God, which counted for so much. Another aspect was prominent to the minds of the primitive Christians, the new environment into which they had passed. The one they had left behind was grim enough.

A great many intelligent Pagans found themselves in a helpless plight, at the time when the Christian mission began to make its appeal. They had long since drifted away from those ancestral religions, whose sway rested on the sanctions of custom more than on anything else. The eclectic tendency, characteristic of the

later philosophy, had extended into the sphere
of religion. The older bonds of tradition had
lost their force. The mental atmosphere which
these **Pagans** breathed had changed. There had
been no definite struggle between old and new.
A generation had grown up whom the Olympian
mythology could no longer interest. The first
attempt at adjustment to the altered condition
of affairs was the reduction of the figures of
famous deities like Zeus, Hera, Apollo, and others
to personified abstractions, which did not, at
least, offend their intellectual presuppositions.
Alongside of this re-interpretation of the
traditional beliefs, other competitors had come
forward to claim men's allegiance. The rude
worship of Dionysus, who stood for the principle
of growth, fertility, life, had in various combinations, disclosed profounder elements of religious aspiration, ideals which searched and
probed men's hearts. The Orphic brotherhoods
who by their ritual and doctrine of purification,
were aiming at a blessed future of immortality, which meant likeness to the Divine,
had never lost their hold, although their influence seemed to spread secretly rather than
in public. The Mystery-religions, which united
spectacular " dances " with spiritual assurances
fitted to meet men's needs, were becoming
more and more popular. This phase of worship had long been known in the Hellenic world
through the famous state-cult at Eleusis, near
Athens, which seems to have absorbed Dionysiac

elements and fused them with a much ruder
strain of thought, producing ultimately a more
refined type of belief, more or less capable of
raising human desires. The Mystery-religions,
having their birth for the most part in Oriental
soil, carried with them many of their indigenous
elements, although, as a rule, they were strongly
influenced if not moulded by Greek forces, as
they took their place in the Hellenistic world.[1]

Those who were comforted by them felt,
at least, that they were not superficial. Some
of their constituents might be crude enough,
allowing their barbaric descent to shine through.
But certain features were of a more uplifting
character. Thus, they developed the idea of
religious association : of a life of brotherhood
in following exalted aims. The conception of
equality in a common religious service was
transforming, and, on the whole, it found
scope in their cults. Further, they professed
to meet the craving for salvation which had
become so prevalent in that epoch. It may
be very difficult to define this widespread
idea. It did not always mean the deliverance
of the individual. The notion of the community as the religious unit still asserted itself.
But we know that, as the result of the disinte-
gration of political life under Alexander the
Great and his successors, the fortunes of the
individual came to take a place in ancient
thought which they had never occupied before.

[1] See Note VII., "*Hellenic*" and "*Hellenistic*," p. 84.

So that probably it was the salvation (σωτηρία) of the individual that chiefly filled their minds. But this salvation meant far more than deliverance from earthly ills, although it certainly included them.

Perhaps it would be rash to conclude that the Pagan world of St. Paul's day knew that which corresponded to our " sense of sin." The literature indicates rather a sense of need, a consciousness of the futility of human strivings in presence of such forces as Fate (εἱμαρμένη), Necessity (ἀναγκή), Chance (τυχή). Multitudes felt the pressure of a leaden burden, and because they could not account for it on any other lines, they came to think of it as a supernatural power. There prevailed a strange mixture of beliefs in the activity of good and evil powers. Some of those beliefs were closely associated with another phase of semi-religious, semi-philosophical thought, which for convenience sake we may call pre-Christian Gnosticism. This was a widely-different cast of attitude, independent of country, race or hereditary creed. It certainly involved a higher view of God than that current in contemporary Paganism. Its professed aim was, as the name indicates, to *know* (γνωστικοί) God and to attain Redemption through that knowledge. But the knowledge striven after was no mere intellectual attainment : it meant that knowledge which comes from spiritual fellowship. The Gnostics were most catholic in their tastes.

They surveyed all forms of belief and worship, and assimilated that which appealed to them. Probably common to all of them was a belief in the evil of matter, and the conception of a necessarily imperfect universe under the ultimate sway of a perfectly good God. Their view of the situation landed them in sheer Dualism, which was buttressed by some of the tendencies of ancient religious thought.

The later Gnostics of the Christian Church tried to reconcile the opposing forces by the notion of a chain of Aeons or Emanations, proceeding from the Divine Nature, losing purity as they approached the world, but finally constituting a bridge between the perfect and the imperfect. We cannot tell whether such a speculation was of influence in the minds of pre-Christian Gnostics. But we know that they were open to every theory which might help towards a unified view of things.

The Judaism of the first century B.C. was deeply saturated both with angelology and demonology. How far that was the result of Persian influence it is impossible to determine. Many contemporary thinkers ascribed life to the starry heavens, to the planets and the fixed stars, a life directly interested in men. This indeed had become the blossoming-time of astrology. The deepest concern was felt for the constellations under which individuals were born. The reading of horoscopes became a most lucrative profession.

It would be extremely hard to draw any strict boundary between some of the beliefs I have mentioned and the practice of magic. So we are not surprised to find magical elements mixed up with them. Magic was especially used in order to gain control over the power of the most important deities. If only their proper *names* were known, the necessary influence could be attained, and the worshipper could count on their favour and help.

People who lived in the kind of atmosphere I have tried to sketch, when they took it seriously, must have been overpowered by mastering fears. What they thought of a religion would mainly consist in the effort to propitiate the gods of whom they were in greatest dread. The supreme aim was to keep on their favourable side, having them for friends and not for foes. Obviously they could have no confidence in any rule of events. The conception of Providence was, indeed, weighty in some philosophical circles, and its influence must have touched the general life. But to the average person, more especially those who had never completely left out of sight the dark Chthonian [1] deities, and still rendered them silent worship, life seemed to be hemmed in by implacable and always incalculable powers, whose delight it was to afflict frail mortals.

These constituted the type of people to whom the Christian Gospel was addressed.

[1] See Note VIII., *Chthonian Worship*, p. 85.

Curiously enough, his Epistles do not contain samples of St. Paul's regular misssionary preaching, but we can gather from the New Testament writings as a whole what these " delegates " of Jesus Christ must have proclaimed.

Probably we ought to say that one of its most valuable features was its indissoluble connection with a Person. The best education for mind or spirit must be concrete. The Old Testament scriptures provided a masterly example of this. Abstractions were everywhere avoided. In the profoundest discussions, the *living* God formed the centre. Unquestionably there comes a stage when you are compelled to use terms which refuse to be translated into vivid images : and the danger is that they may be forced into frames for which they are not intended. But to grasp a longing, simple heart, you are obliged to speak in vivid pictures. It was of incalculable advantage to the early community that many were still living who had " companied with Jesus." There could scarcely be imagined a position more alien to the early Christian than that which despises or ignores historical facts. Most of them had listened with reverence to the Synagogue-lessons from the Old Testament. These belonged to a record of the Divine training of a people. They were essentially historical. Even the messages of the prophets and psalmists grew out of a definitely concrete setting. The starting-point of the Gospel was a Man who had lived a real human life in Palestine : had mixed with men and women as their Brother : had shared their ordinary needs and trials : had finally been sentenced to a criminal's death. The disciples had been roused from despair to great gladness by the assurance that their Master had triumphed over death, and was alive for evermore. Especially the kind of experience which had come to them enforced that assurance. All their hopes and joys circled round a living Person, of whose presence they were continually conscious.

But, as the Synoptic gospels show, by far the most significant event in Jesus' career, in the judgment of the early community, was His death on the Cross. That event and its associations occupy a larger place in these documents than anything else. It is equally prominent, as has been hinted, in the Epistles addressed to Christian societies. This is not at all accounted for by the shock it caused Jesus' disciples and friends. We know how it must have hindered many devout Jews from identifying themselves immediately with the early group of believers. We are left in no doubt as to the manner in which it struck the Apostles and their friends. To all it was the crowning instance of self-sacrificing love. Both Acts and the Epistles give evidence of the various lines on which its religious significance was explained, but it may probably be said with truth that these explanations are over-

shadowed by the marvellous disposition embodied in the crucified Jesus. That they can
never forget. At that they can never cease
to wonder. This is the love of God in His Son,
a love which "passeth knowledge." Here is
the creation of an atmosphere for the new
religion. I am inclined to think that the
creation of this new atmosphere was in many
respects the most wonderful thing that Christianity ever accomplished. Indeed, its consequences have never had full scope. No justice
has been done to them in the modern world.
To be convinced that the problem of the universe *has been solved* : that it is possible for
men and women to enter the real presence of
the living God, and to find Him not as cold
Power or Law but as a loving Father ; that
is the sorest load lifted off human hearts.
Here lies the supreme fact of the Forgiveness
of Sins. We know that Jesus served Himself
heir to the great movement inaugurated by
the Baptist, whose special watchword was
"repentance, with a view to the forgiveness
of sins." We know that one of the features
of His mission which first shocked the Scribes
and Pharisees was His claim to forgive sins.
He uttered this claim as the Son of Man, the
dispenser of the Kingdom of God. Forgiveness
belonged to the very essence of His Messiahship.
And those who met Him at this point felt that
they were in touch with the very heart of God.
All through the history of the Christian mission,

Baptism, the entrance into the life of the community, was the symbol of forgiveness. And Ritschl has good reason to urge that the Church was essentially the society of the forgiven. St. Paul himself assigns a far more prominent place to the conception than might appear on the surface, as, when he speaks of being justified, he practically means the same thing as forgiveness.

We can see, therefore, what happened. Jews and Gentiles were offered Love in exchange for Fear. I have purposely grouped together Jews and Gentiles, although I recognise how much more spiritual the Jewish view of God actually was. But fear had a real place in it : fear of failing to meet the Divine requirements, of neglecting the full demands of the Law, of violating the reverence due to God by approaching Him too freely. " You," says Paul, writing to the members of the Christian community at Rome, which embraced Jews as well as Gentiles, and having all the time in his thoughts the attitude of Jews, " You did not receive the spirit of slavery relapsing into fear, but you received the spirit of sonship, in which we cry, Abba, *i.e.* Father " (Rom. viii. 15). That was the renewing process. The ideal which the most spiritual both among Jews and Gentiles set before them, had been once for all realised. Goodness, truth, and the Messianic Hope had all been summed up in Jesus of Nazareth, the promised Messiah of God.

Now these facts had endless significance. Perhaps we sometimes wonder why so large a place is given in the Christian documents of the New Testament to the Messiah. Perhaps we are inclined to regard this as merely a survival of Judaism. But even for Judaism the Messianic idea was no empty form. It was packed with contents. Without lingering to discuss the conception fully, it may at once be said that no more suitable link could have been found to unite God's dealings in the past with those in the present : to unify the religious history of the Jewish people. It is true that in Jesus the Kingdom of God proved to be much wider than Judaism. But we must remember that the heritage of the Old Testament was uniquely rich, and it was through their Messianic associations that the Gentile Christians could assert their claims to that wonderful heritage. The pious in Israel had for centuries looked forward to the time when God should vindicate His people through His servant, the Messiah. And Apocalyptic thought, which contained the most vital strains in the religion of its time, regarded that epoch as the introduction of a new spiritual order.

One of the chief problems for early Christianity was the blending of the old order with the new. It was not easy to conceive their precise relationship. Perhaps we come nearest the truth in saying that they regarded the Messianic Age as having projected itself upon the present. In the Fourth Gospel there is no present and future. The antithesis lies between the " earthly " and the " heavenly," the " visible " and the " invisible." But we can discern a common point of view from the words of Hebrews vi. 5, where the author speaks of those " who have tasted the excellent word of God and *the powers of the coming age.*" These powers have anticipated all popular expectation. The crucial mark of their presence is the working of the Holy Spirit in the hearts of believers. Already those who are linked to the exalted Lord by faith have an endowment which equips them for any situation.

Note VII

" Hellenic " and " Hellenistic "

These terms have been repeatedly used in the course of our discussion. It may be advisable to define more closely what is meant. The adjective " Hellenic " is employed roughly to describe what is essentially *Greek* in character. Having its origin in the famous world of thought and activity which we associate with such states as Athens, and such men as Thucydides, the great Athenian dramatist, Æschylus, Sophocles, and Euripides, the philosophers Socrates and Plato, it denotes the kind of influence which flowed out from the activities we connect with such men.

Perhaps it is more difficult to define " Hellenistic." But, generally speaking, the world which
was built up on the foundations of Alexander's
conquests may be called the " Hellenistic "
world. That meant a civilisation symbolised
by the diffusion of the Greek language and by
the adoption of that larger point of view
which had its roots in earlier Greek life, but
failed to preserve that older influence in its
purity, having been contaminated at various
points by semi-Greek and Oriental modes of
thought, feeling, and custom. Hence it includes those elements prominent in Græco-
Roman provinces, like Asia, Egypt, and Syria,
which while professing to be Greek, continually revealed traces of indigenous ideas and
practices, overlaid with a thin veneer of
Hellenism.

Note VIII

Chthonian Worship

We should receive a false conception of
Greek religion in the epoch we are considering,
if we left out of sight a phase of belief which is
never prominent in literature but which is
none the less potent in influence.

In all civilisations there is an ancient element
which shows an extraordinary persistence and
discloses the amazing power of animistic ideas.
We know the place occupied by ancestor-
worship in the earliest phases of primitive

religion.   Sepulchral usages were peculiarly
significant in such epochs.   And the spirits
of the dead which were then propitiated seem
to have been combined with sombre earth-
spirits and deities of the nether world.
Numerous popular superstitions, charms, and
spells circled round these gloomy forces.   The
worship of them seldom comes into the light.
But dark hints occur here and there of this
sway.   People shrink from speaking of them.
This cult is largely carried on in secret.   But
far more genuine influence is really assigned to
them than to the more splendid deities, the
artistic representations of which was the wonder
of the Greek world.   Possibly we may thus
partly account for the appeal which the mystery-
cults made to Greek minds.   In any case, we
can better understand the place occupied by
demon-worship when the Christian mission
began to be proclaimed.

QUESTIONS FOR DISCUSSION.

1. By what means did the Greek-speaking world of St
   Paul's day seek religious satisfaction ?
2. What element of failure was common to Pagans and Jews ?
3. Why was the cross central in Christian thought and
   preaching ?
4. What was gained by preaching Jesus as the Christ ?

FOR FURTHER READING.

The Christ of Revolution.   By J. R. Coates.
Roman Society from Nero to Marcus Aurelius, pp. 547–584.
   By Sir S. Dill.

CHAPTER VII

THE SECOND COMING

1 Thess. iv., v. ; 2 Thess. i., ii. ; Dan. vii. ; Phil. iv. ; John iii.

In the preceding paragraphs I have tried to emphasise the value for Christianity of the Messianic Hope. We have seen how it bound together Old Testament and New in the only fashion that we could conceive to be profitable. Most Christian communities, in the early days of the enterprise, started from the Synagogue. That is to say, their associations were predominantly Jewish, and there can be little question that the identification of Jesus with the patiently-awaited Anointed of God was of immense assistance in the transition from the old faith to the new.

I do not mean to suggest that the Christian Messiah directly exemplified the Jewish conception. There were far-reaching modifications. Perhaps the chief of these was one which lay at the basis of the early Christian community, that Jesus had reached His exalted place along the path of suffering. The Jewish theology had left no room for this. Its Messianic figure, with His Divine attributes, was exclusively a regal, judicial Being. The note of His activity was victory, and never failure. But

Jesus appears, from His early days, to have identified Himself with the Servant of the Lord in Deutero-Isaiah. He thereby humbled Himself, was willing to face scorn and contradiction for the sake of His vocation, finally, " to bear the sins of many " (Isa. liii. 12). Moreover, the current belief in Judaism was the coming once for all of the Messiah, after a time of varied preparation, to claim His Kingdom and to establish it in righteousness. The Christian believer recognised that Messiah had come in Jesus of Nazareth, but that one day He should return in power and great glory.

Probably many are surprised that the Second Advent of Jesus should take so prominent a place in the New Testament documents. We ourselves find it so difficult to adjust the idea of our Lord's return to our inborn conception of the gradual progress of the race, the social diffusion of the Kingdom of God, the unification of the world by moral and religious influence. Especially are we startled by the conviction common to so many of the early Christians that the Second Advent should come soon. It seems impossible to doubt that that was the impression received by the first disciples from Jesus' own words. What did He mean ? I think we are apt to throw into the centre of the discussion that which preplexes us most, the predicted nearness of His coming. I do not intend to point out the lack of harmony between such a position and many of the implications of His teaching. But I doubt whether He was much concerned about the chronological aspect of the situation. If we are to search for explanations of His manner of speech, perhaps it is best to look for this in the prophetic and apocalyptic habit of announcing as near those results of which the speaker is certain. In any case, the focal elements in Jesus' teaching are entirely independent of the chronological aspect of His return. He came the first time to invite men and women into His Father's family. They were summoned to enter now, and to receive all the privileges which God intended for them. There could not be a *better* condition than this citizenship available for them, this welcome into the fellowship of God which embodied the highest end in religion. So that we must place the favourite question as to the " when " of the Kingdom at the circumference and not at the centre of the teaching of Jesus. Nevertheless, enough has been said to show the remarkable place which Eschatology, the doctrine of the Events of the End, occupied in the minds of the earliest believers. Let us try to estimate the significance of this.

It came natural to Jewish Christians to lay strong emphasis on the Last Things. Apart altogether from the teaching of Jesus, their thoughts had moved for long among such interests as the resurrection, the judgment,

the Messiah, the Consummation of the Kingdom
of God. I do not turn aside to secondary
conceptions such as that of the Millennium.[1]
Their ideas were highly pictorial, and we are
still apt to clothe our thoughts of these things
in their pictures. They were accustomed to
follow a recognised series of stages in these
extraordinary phenomena. They started with
a definite scheme, and abode by it more or less
rigidly. That they followed older traditions
is evident, if we note how St Paul's eschatological descriptions regularly approximate to
those of the Prophets. Nothing is more in-
structive in this connection than a careful examination of the marginal references in First
and Second Thessalonians, the specially eschatological epistles among his writings.
Probably the Jewish section of the church
clung tenaciously to its scheme, even when its
literal hopes seemed to be falsified. The remarkable point is that as the days went on,
St Paul seems to become less and less definite
in his forecasts. He never indeed lost sight
of the Lord's return. But when, in one of the
latest of his Epistles, "Philippians," he enjoins
upon his readers the importance of a gracious,
reasonable disposition, and adds as a motive,
"the Lord is near" (iv. 5), we can discover
that he has ceased to deal with pictures.
Indeed, one may say, that as his life and work
advance, his eschatology may be summed up

---

[1] See Note IX., *The Millennium*, p. 96.

in the idea of Hope. He is content to do without definitions, and to leave the future conditions vague and blurred.

Possibly the converts from Paganism were never so concrete in their delineations of the End as the Jewish Christians. In effect, this whole sphere of conceptions lay to a large extent outside their native thought. For the Hellenic idea of history was entirely distinct from the Jewish. The Greeks did not possess the notion of continuous progress up to a definite goal. They thought of history as a succession of long cycles of experiences, repeated over and over again. There was no place for a consummation. Yet before now their deeper religious speculations were largely occupied with the notion of life beyond the grave. In more primitive days those who reflected on immortality were probably naïve enough in their expectations. As reflection advanced, the spiritual aspect of the future life became more and more dominant. But on that ground a missionary like St Paul was quite prepared to meet his Greek hearers. For the Christian doctrine of the Last Things became more and more completely spiritualised. This formed part of the general movement away from the national to the spiritual. We have that movement exemplified on almost every page of the Fourth Gospel. No more striking instance could be quoted than the author's idea of judgment, as in chap. iii. 18-21 : "This is the judgment, that the light has come into the world, and men loved the darkness rather than the light, for their deeds were evil."

How, then, did Eschatology *tell* in the early Christian community ? Recall the circumstances out of which the majority of lives had emerged. Without in any way exaggerating the condition of first-century Paganism, we can discover from the pages of any writer who has summarised the extant evidence that life in the Roman Empire was gross enough. The creed of the multitude was : " Let us eat and drink, for to-morrow we die." Wealth had accumulated, and at the other extreme, poverty [1] The bridled self-will was the chief principle of action. Religion, as a rule, was a form of State-cult and superficial tradition. The universe seemed to be governed by various incalculable forces, whose sway was relentless. There was scarcely any outlet for energy in the political sphere, for policy had really become a matter for the imperial will. The frescoes unearthed at the excavation of Pompeii give a rough general notion of the prevailing tone of life. It might be described in the words of 1 John ii. 16 : " The lust of the flesh and the lust of the eyes and the vainglory of possessions." The current ideals were unblushingly materialistic. Impurity of all sorts was con-

---

[1] See L. Friedländer, *Roman Life and Manners under the Early Empire*, passim.

doned. The relation between the sexes was, as a whole, most dissolute. Frightful rapacity had become rampant. The only expedient plan for ruling the people was " bread and the games." Even people of higher aims winked at iniquity. Again and again, in early-Christian literature, the veil is for a moment lifted. " Make no mistake," says St Paul, writing to the restless, self-satisfied Corinthians, " neither fornicators, nor idolaters, nor adulterers, nor effeminate, nor pæderasts, nor thieves, nor swindlers, no drunkards, no slanderers, no extortioners shall inherit the kingdom of God. And this is what some of you were " (1 Cor. vi. 9-10). That kind of atmosphere must have produced its effect. The pages of Diogenes Laertius, although often little more than a collection of gossip, indicate the outlook of many of the philosophers. Scarcely any sanctions existed to curb the prevailing laxity.

Suddenly, those who have yielded to the solemn appeals of the Christian missionaries are brought into contact with a new moral standard. The Golden Rule is set before them. They are reminded of a moral process which goes on in their own lives, the direct result of their conduct. The character of Jesus Christ is made their model. The goal of all their living is righteousness. " You must be perfect," the Master had said, " even as your Father in Heaven is perfect " (Matt. v. 48). The word

" perfect " was regularly used in philosophical discourse of moral flawlessness. It represented the highest stage of spiritual attainment. The Christian aim is likeness to Jesus Christ, through whom the real nature of the living God can be conceived. Only on that condition is there any prospect of entrance into the consummated Divine Kingdom, which Christ shall return to establish. Now, even if they had possessed clearer ideas of the " times and seasons " of these great future events, this would mean unceasing watchfulness and self-control. A backward step was hard to retrieve, and temptations were innumerable. For they were involved at every turn in the life of their contemporaries. No solemnity of conduct was too costly to prepare them for the Second Advent of the Lord. But, in truth, everything lay in obscurity. Nay. The events of the End were likely to be quite sudden and unexpected. " You yourselves," writes St Paul to the Thessalonians, " will know that the Day of the Lord is to come like a thief in the night, when people say, Peace and safety, then sudden destruction assails them, as birth-pangs do the pregnant woman, and they shall not escape. But you, brethren, are not shrouded in darkness, so that the Day shall come upon you like a thief, for you all are sons of the light and sons of the day. . . . Therefore, let us not fall asleep as do others, but let us wake up and live soberly " (1 Thess. v. 2-6).

We inevitably connect these sentences with Jesus' utterance in Matt. xxiv. 42.

A similar strain is found again and again in the New Testament. "Be ready for your King: be prepared to enter His Kingdom." The rationale of it all is forcibly expressed in 1 John ii. 28: "And now, my children, abide in Him, so that when He is revealed, we may have glad fearlessness of bearing ($\pi\alpha\rho\rho\eta\sigma\iota\alpha\nu$), and may not be shamed out of His presence at His coming."

We begin to realise the extraordinary ethical value of this eschatology. It fills the minds of these immature Christians, so lately fettered by the low standards of Paganism, and provides a new and most potent motive for patient watchfulness and prayer. They are impelled to rise above their former moral level. Another type of life is created, one which gradually impresses their Pagan neighbours.

The eschatological impulse seems to have endured for long. It did its part nobly in consolidating the conduct befitting Christians. St Paul, as we have seen, appeals to it even in the latest of his Epistles (Phil. iv. 5). That it was never far distant from his mind is suggested by such passages as 1 Cor. xvi. 22. That letter reveals the Apostle in varying attitudes towards the Corinthians. He has had to rebuke and to congratulate, to answer questions and to lay down rules. He cannot feel satisfied with the complex situation. And now, in the closing paragraph of the document, after finishing his salutation, and before leaving a benediction with the community, Paul interpolates the earnest petition, Μαρὰν ἀθά, "Lord, come." That thought is his supreme refuge from the strife, intrigues, imperfections, and spiritual declension of the members of one of his most important Christian societies.

NOTE IX

The Millennium

The doctrine of the Millennium seems to be a conception conditioned by existing Apocalyptic forecasts. It really serves as a compromise between two prevalent beliefs. The one is that of older Judaism that the consummation of its history will be reached in the rule of Messiah, the Anointed of God, over a purified people, and his victory over all their enemies. But as Apocalyptic thought developed, the belief became prominent that the new, blessed era was to be completely distinguished from the old. No longer was the Messianic reign to be an earthly rule. The Messianic future was to consist in a new *order*. Its conditions were to be supramundane. These two conceptions were allowed to lie side by side, the more material being favoured by the nationalistically inclined among the Jews, the more spiritual by the more essentially apocalyptic party. Apparently, for the sake of compromise, the Millennium was conceived, the notion of a reign of Messiah on earth for a thousand years, before the coming order should be ushered in.

QUESTIONS FOR DISCUSSION.

1. How did early Christian converts differ from their pagan neighbours ?
2. What was the origin of early Christian expectations of the Second Advent ?
3. How were these expectations modified during the first century ?
4. What was the value of them to the early Church ?

FOR FURTHER READING.

Between the Old and New Testaments. By R. H. Charles.
The Messianic Hope in the New Testament, pp. 163–176. By Shailer Mathews.

CHAPTER VIII

THE LORDSHIP OF CHRIST

Phil. ii. ; 1 Cor. viii. ; Rom. vi., x. ; 2 Cor. x. ; John xiii.

WE must further examine the vital energies in the experience of the early community. Careful readers of the Epistles must have observed that these writers love to speak, above all else, of " Our Lord, Jesus Christ," or of, " Jesus Christ, our Lord." This is not the place to dwell on the recent discussions of the title " Lord." [1] It does not seriously affect our purpose whether the title was already current in early Palestinian Christianity or whether it was rather a custom of the Greek-speaking communities on Gentile soil. But it appears to me, without going any further, that its Palestinian origin can only be denied by re-writing the opening section of the Acts of the Apostles which seems to presuppose an early Jewish source. However imperfect the source may be, there is not a particle of real evidence to show that the designation " Lord " was inserted here and there by a redactor. We know that the Septuagint had long since translated one of the Old Testament names for God by *Kyrios* ($\kappa\acute{\upsilon}\rho\iota\upsilon\varsigma$), " Lord." We are pre-

[1] See Note X., *Jesus Christ as Lord*, p. 109.

pared by the testimony of Epistles, Gospels, and Acts for believing that after the early disciples were convinced of Jesus' resurrection, they applied to Him this remarkable designation of worship. For these all-important sources agree in their testimony that the living Jesus was for His followers the spring of Divine power. The fresh endowment of spiritual energy and enthusiasm which they called the gift of the Holy Spirit corroborates that view. A most interesting incidental piece of testimony is found in 1 Cor. xvi. 22, the passage discussed at the close of our last chapter. There St Paul uses not the ordinary Greek but the Aramaic phrase. The only reason that can be adduced is that the phase *Maran Atha* carried a special solemnity in itself, as consecrated by the usage of the earliest Aramaic-speaking communities which would certainly be Palestinian. To attribute the origin of such a phrase to any bilingual society of the Diaspora is a refuge of despair.

The ascription of the term " Lord " to Jesus is nothing less than an ascription of worship. In one of his most difficult paragraphs St Paul makes that quite clear. Urging unity of mind and spirit upon his Philippian converts, and deprecating all strife and vain-glory, he holds up to them the example of the mind of Christ, " who, being in the form of God, did not regard equality with God as a prize to be snatched, but emptied himself in taking the form of a

slave, being born in the likeness of men. And
having been formed in fashion as a man, he
humbled himself, becoming obedient as far as
death, even the death of the cross. Where-
fore God also exalted him, and gave him the
name which is above every name, so that in
the name of Jesus every knee might bow of
things in heaven and on earth and under the
earth, and that every tongue might confess
that Jesus Christ is *Lord*, to the glory of God
the Father " (Phil. ii. 6–11). No one who care-
fully examines the thought can be in doubt
that " the name which is above every name "
is that of " Lord." Jesus is thereby put on
an equality with God before all the universe.
God can demand nothing higher than worship
and reverence and all that they involve. That
also is the pinnacle which these early believers
feel that Jesus has reached according to the
determination of the Divine purpose. The
marvellous thing is that He has reached it
along the pathway of suffering, shame, and
death. Humility is the most powerful energy
in the Son of the living God.

Now there was evidently universal agreement in the early Christian society as to the
Lordship of Jesus Christ. How much did it
mean for the believers of the first century ? It
is legitimate to illustrate the situation from
Pagan religion, although I totally reject the
hypothesis that there was an organic connection
between the two phases at this point. We

know that in this epoch in various Asiatic cults, there was a sharp distinction often drawn between " gods " and " lords " in the description of deities. Some scholars hold that this distinction applied to St Paul's word in 1 Cor. viii. 5. It is just possible that that may be so, but in any case the distinction stood for something. The term " gods " was used of the ancient Olympian deities, who still remained at the centre of the State-cults, while " lord " was applied to those more human objects of worship involved in the Mystery-religions, as, e.g. Attis, in the rites of the Great Mother. Although in a sense " lord " might be considered on a lower level than " god," the homage given to the former was more heartfelt, as the being thus designated had shared in human experience. The relation to him seemed more intimate and genuine. This fact may have paved the way for the ready recognition of the Lordship of Christ among Pagan converts. It seems needless to suppose that this had its origin in the cult-necessities of Hellenistic communities, which had been accustomed to the practice I have mentioned. The situation as previously sketched is quite sufficient to account for the usage. One important implication of the conception is its obvious nexus with Old Testament ways of thinking. Again and again the writers of the Psalms call themselves " slaves " of God In these passages the word " slave " had assumed a religious connotation. A

similar situation appears in the prophets. The
New Testament Epistles, whose keynote we
have seen to be freedom, often adopt the term
" slave " as the correlative of Jesus' title
" Lord." The usage implied that the followers
of the Lord were His possession, His property,
and indeed that was symbolised by the very
ritual of Baptism. An inevitable consequence
was that the disciple regarded himself as completely at the disposal of his Master. His will
was spiritually merged in that of the living
" Lord." He was pledged to deny himself.
There was also involved the idea that the
" slave " was under the protection, the guar-
dianship of his *Kyrios*. Here we have a conception which completely tallies with Old
Testament thought. It was easy to convert
this earlier idea into the spiritual habit of thinking in the New Testament. And it is one of
many evidences of the incomparable value for
the early community of having the Old Testament as its great authoritative document.
That was merely incidental. The supreme
worth lay in the conviction that the living
Christ was above all : that the fortunes both of
the community and of individual believers were
in His hands : that they could say, " The Lord
is my Shepherd," with an accent which had
never been heard before. Here was the ground
of the confidence with which they were able to
confront an inhospitable environment. It was
no longer a dull, incalculable struggle with

opposing forces, but an advance to victory through the Lord of all. Again, the very essence of a slave's duty was obedience. Now, at a very early stage, the tendency appears to make Christ a new legislator : to regard the Sermon on the Mount, *e.g.* as a freshly-promulgated code of laws which should take the place in the lives of Christians of the Law of Moses. This was really one of the germs of Roman Catholicism in the shape it has since assumed. Men were to exchange one set of rules affecting the spiritual life for another. To take up such a position was to deny that on which leaders like St Paul laid the emphasis. The joy of his supreme religious discovery was involved in the abolishing of legislation.

But that transformation was attended by all manner of perils which did not take long to show themselves. Even in St Paul's lifetime we have hints of people who claimed licence of action because they were not subjected to a definite law, but within a realm of grace. The Apostle has no patience with such claims. Taking an extreme case he asks : " Shall we continue in sin that grace may abound ? " And he spurns the objection with horror : " God forbid " (Rom. vi. 1). No one knew better the necessity of some standard or pattern of ethical life. It would have been sheer folly in dealing with these immature Pagan converts to have ignored the need. And he has no difficulty in showing that a spiritual connexion with Christ must imply the same attitude as His towards sin (Rom. vi. 2-23). Looked at under the aspect which we have been considering in the present chapter, the new attitude, the only conceivable attitude, of him who calls Christ Lord is obedience to His will.

That was, of course, the most difficult task set before members of the early community. It was difficult largely because Christ did not promulgate a new set of regulations, but rather threw out certain proposed principles by which a Christian life should be ruled. The application of principles to details is always hard. What made it at all possible in the primitive society was the actual record of the life of Jesus to which they could refer. To begin with, it is probable that they came to understand that life through the medium of their missionaries. It is worthy of note, *e.g.* that St Paul urges them to become imitators of him as he is of Christ (1 Cor. xi. 1). This is true to human life. Experienced missionaries still tell us that their lives have to be the interpretation of the higher life to newly-won, simple converts. Just as they have been ambassadors in Christ's behalf, so must they attempt to be practical expositors of His conduct. Thus, in his earliest letter, St Paul reminds the Thessalonians that they had become imitators of him and of the Lord (1 Thess. i. 6).

We can scarcely doubt that the new ethical

standard by which the early Christians sought
to regulate their lives formed the most impressive appeal to those acquainted with
them. We have already discussed some of its
consequences : especially the spirit of mutual
love and service which characterised their
conduct in the most varying situations. But
some of the incidental appeals in the New Testament remind us of the width of range that
was involved. Take, *e.g.* 2 Cor. x. 1 : "For
my part, I Paul beseech you by the meekness
and gracious reasonableness of Christ." Here is
the disposition which alone can hope to deal
fairly with a situation. It means the laying
aside of prejudices, the assuming of two sides
to a question, the willingness to put yourself
in your opponent's place, the control of passion
and bitterness, the remembrance of the inevitable frailty and fallibility of human judgment,
the readiness to search for the rights of the case.
Think of what this implied for men and women
thrust by the necessities of daily life and business into innumerable complex situations.
We have pictures of what constantly happened
in the First Epistle to the Corinthian community. A supreme *crux* for those who had
become converts was their inevitable connection
and association with the Pagan society to
which they had belonged. Paul is consulted
on the subject of the proper attitude towards
sacrificial meat, towards mixed marriages,
towards slavery in Pagan households. Certain

positions would commend themselves to particular temperaments, which would work injury on both sides. Some would call for no compromise. Others would be too willing to acommodate themselves to inevitable circumstances. Others still would be attracted by a mood of superiority, which viewed these controverted points as matters of indifference. Such a counsel as that quoted above seemed precisely to hit the mean.

Then there was the large question of the relation of the sexes. At this period, public opinion was exceedingly lax. The Christian missionaries recognised that any uncertainty on such a subject would be fatal to the new faith, for chastity lay at the basis of all right views of the family and of society. To hesitate there would be to cut the very roots of wholesome life. Hence, the early missionaries make their position unmistakable : *e.g.* 1 Cor. vi. 15 : " Do you not know that your bodies are members of Christ ? Shall I then take the members of Christ and make them the members of a harlot ? God forbid." This instance reminds us of the fundamental fashion in which they deal with the perplexities.

Now it is obvious that the transformed moral outlook must have had the most divergent results. New doctrines can be more easily grasped than new ethical standards. It was a simpler matter to appreciate the gift of the Holy Spirit or to be convinced that Jesus was alive for evermore than completely to change one's manner of living. Men's minds were athirst for more satisfying conceptions of the relation of heaven to earth. But their ordinary conduct was hemmed in by a network of customs, traditions, and practices whose meshes were hard to cut. We are not, therefore, surprised by Professor von Dobschütz's view based upon the various types of evidence, that, while the Christians of the second century hardly seem to have grasped some of St Paul's profound ideas, their standard of morals was much more stable and secure than that of the earlier generation of converts. It must be a tardy process to cut one's self loose from a group of habits which have accumulated through centuries.

On the other hand, the new conduct was a far more direct challenge to the established system of things than any new creed. It must have, more than any other cause, marked off the early believers from their neighbours. That is to say, it would be the chief instrument in provoking opposition. People invariably recognise in a higher level of action a criticism of their own standards, and they resent it. That accounts for much of the hatred and scorn which the early community had to endure, and the cruel persecutions through which it had to pass. But who can doubt that the actual behaviour of those who called Christ Lord must have been the most powerful stimulus to re-

flective minds, the most telling witness to the
faith that could confront the outside world ?
The truth is, as Harnack points out (*op. cit.*
I. p. 208 f.) that " all the [Christian] apologists
rely on the fact that even their opponents hold
goodness to be good and wickedness to be evil.
They consider it superfluous to waste their time
in proving that goodness is really goodness ;
they can be sure of assent to this proposition.
What they seek to prove is that goodness among
Christians is not an impotent claim or a pale
ideal, but a power which is developed on all sides
and actually exercised in life. It was of special
importance to them to be able to show . . .
that what was weak and poor and ignoble rose
thereby to strength and worth."

In the light of what has been said, we can
appreciate the injunction of Ignatius to the
Christians at Ephesus : " Suffer them to learn a
lesson at least from your deeds. Be meek when
they break out in anger ; be lowly in return
for their vaunting words, set your prayers
against their blasphemies. . . . Be not zealous
to imitate them in requital. Let us show
ourselves their brethren by our gracious reasonableness, and let us be zealous to be imitators
of the Lord." (10, quoted by Harnack, *op.
cit.* I. p. 210, n. 1.)

Note X

Jesus Christ as Lord

One of the central discussions in New Testament scholarship at the present time relates to the title of "Lord" given to Jesus Christ in the early community. No term is so typical of the attitude of the Epistles to the risen Jesus. Indeed St Paul's language in Phil. ii. 9 reminds us that this was the highest designation given to him, that which marked him out as the object of worship. In correspondence with this, St Paul often calls himself the "slave" of Christ.

How did this usage arise ? We are told by scholars like Bousset that it belongs originally to Hellenistic communities, consisting of Diaspora Jews and Pagans. They were familiar with the deities of Mystery-cults, who, in contrast with the gods of the Olympian pantheon ($\theta\epsilon o i$), were usually known as $\kappa\acute{\upsilon}\rho\iota o\varsigma$. Jesus, as adored by the community, as the supreme object of worship, is $\kappa\acute{\upsilon}\rho\iota o\varsigma$. It is really in the midst of community life that the worship of Jesus begins.

But there seems good reason to place the beginnings of the usage further back. The main drift of the Synoptic Gospels suggests, when taken along with the earlier chapters of Acts, that the worship of Jesus belongs at least to the earliest Palestinian Christianity. Now, if we give its full force to the impression made by Jesus on His original followers, we need not be surprised that they should come to ascribe to Him a term closely associated in the LXX. with the Messianic hopes of the Old Testament. We know the extraordinary place taken in the early Church by such passages as Ps. cx. 1 : "The Lord said unto my Lord, Sit thou on my right hand until I make thy foes thy footstool." Such a statement was bound to suggest the title κύριος for the Christian Messiah. And the tendency to adopt it would be intensified by the fact that κύριος had been used in the LXX. to translate one of the Divine names.

We have an incidental proof of the age and *habitat* of the title. In the closing paragraph of 1 Corinthians, St Paul gives vent to the devout ejaculation, μάραν ἀθά : "Our Lord is coming." Why does he here, as so rarely, adopt an Aramaic phrase in the midst of his Greek letter ? Surely it can be nothing else than the reminiscence of a favourite phrase in Palestinian Church worship, which was, of course, carried on in Aramaic. Paul could recall the solemn conviction with which in that worship the words were uttered. They must have taken a prominent place in the thought of the early community to be in the forefront of their worship. And the casual allusion reminds us that they formed an integral part of the life of the earliest type of Jewish Christianity.

QUESTIONS FOR DISCUSSION.

1. What did the early Christians mean by calling Jesus "Lord"?
2. What was involved in being a "slave" of Jesus Christ?
3. Discuss the relative importance of doctrine and conduct.
4. What are the essentials of a Christian disposition?
5. Why is chastity imperative for a Christian?

FOR FURTHER READING.

The Environment of Early Christianity. By S. Angus.
The Theology of the Epistles, pp. 22–27, 82–86. By H. A. A. Kennedy.

CHAPTER IX

THE GRACE OF GOD

Rom. xii. ; Gal. v. ; Eph. i. ; Phil. i. ; Heb. ii., xi.

AT the outset, I tried to emphasise the nature of the atmosphere in which the early community had its true beginnings. We saw that its chief feature was the presence and power of the Holy Spirit. Many descriptions might be given of that remarkable endowment. It might justly be called the Divine response to the individual's faith in Christ, taking faith in its large, Pauline sense of complete surrender of body and spirit to the risen Lord. The results of its operation were manifold. That which St Paul most highly valued was the sense of a wonderful Divine basis for daily living, which expressed itself in such qualities as " love, joy, peace, long-suffering, graciousness, kindness, trust-worthiness, meekness, self-control " (Gal. v. 22, 23). The Apostle placed these qualities high above the abnormal equipment so eagerly coveted, *e.g.* at Corinth (*cf.* 1 Cor. xii. 4–11, 28–30). That equipment might mean aptness to deal with complex situations in the Church's life, comprehension of the profoundest spiritual truth, the heroic kind of faith which Jesus had commended, power to heal and to perform other wonderful works, the capacity for effective preaching, ability to " speak with tongues " or to interpret them. There is no doubt that these unique endowments made an immense impression on the heathen world. It is impossible for us to estimate them precisely. Spiritual power is one of the most impalpable and elusive of the potent personal forces in the universe. That the missionaries took its presence for granted is clear from such passages as Rom. xv. 18 : " I shall not venture to tell of any of the things which Christ did not accomplish through me, to win the obedience of the heathen, by word and by deed, by the force of miracles and marvels, by the power of the Holy Spirit," and 2 Cor. xii. 12 (Moffatt): " You had all the miracles that mark an apostle done for you fully and patiently—miracles, wonders and deeds of power." These references are quite incidental, and they evidently do not call up matters of controversy. What the Apostle included under them we have no means of judging. We discover that several centuries later the scornful antagonist of Christianity, Celsus, regarded the power of exorcising demons as one of the most remarkable testimonies to the faith which he despised. We are at liberty to suppose that actions which St Paul classed among " miracles " we might to-day place under a very different category if we knew all the circumstances. It has, further, become plain in the course of our investigation that the environment of this gift of spiritual power was something new and unheard of. We may call it *the atmosphere of the Divine Grace.* It is of vast importance to discover what this meant and what it led to. We are aware that the idea of the shepherding care of God belongs to Old Testament religion and naturally passed over into early Christian thought. We have also recognised that a doctrine of Providence, self-evident to a Jew, formed a vital element in that later Greek philosophy, which was religion rather than metaphysical speculation. All such beliefs characterised the position of devout men, whether within or outside the early community. But something undreamed of had asserted itself in the minds of all who took up a serious attitude towards Jesus Christ and His Gospel. They were convinced that God had instituted a new order of relationship to the world of human life and conduct. This was an order of faith, hope, and love. The most remarkable feature was that nothing in the process of history directly accounted for it. Not that they supposed it to be a meaningless break. St Paul invariably recognises that the moment had come for fresh initiative : *e.g.* Gal. iv. 4. " Now when the fulness of the time came, God sent forth His Son." [1] But this passage brings out his real standpoint. The transforming action in human history was *God's* doing. It was not the natural

---

[1] See Note XI., *The Fulness of the Time*, p. 119.

culmination of a regularly-working evolution. It was sudden and unexpected. And throughout the life of Jesus it kept operating on the same lines. Jesus Himself recognised the fresh departure : *e.g.* Luke x. 23–24 : "And he turned to his disciples and said to them privately, Blessed are the eyes which see the things that ye see ; for I tell you that many prophets and kings desired to see those things which ye see, and did not see them ; and to hear those things which ye hear, and did not hear them."

Now this condition was not interrupted by the departure of Jesus. We have discovered how thereafter the disciples entered upon an exuberant spiritual life. That life spread. To quote Acts ii. 47 : "The Lord was adding [to the community] those that were daily being saved." Whatever secondary causes might be assigned a place in what was happening, Divine mercy was behind it all. This discloses the regular apostolic standpoint. *Cf.* Ephes. ii. 8, 9 : "By grace you have been saved through faith : that is not your own doing, the gift is God's." Such a passage shows clearly the importance of Divine grace. It is very significant that the word in the Old Testament which stands nearest "grace," (*chesed*) is scarcely ever in the Septuagint rendered by the favourite New Testament term *charis* ($\chi \acute{a} \rho \iota s$) but almost invariably and a great many times by *eleos* ($\check{\epsilon} \lambda \epsilon o s$), which is comparatively rare in the Epistles, and seldom used by St Paul. That implies that " grace " in its New Testament sense is practically a later phenomenon. Indeed it might almost be called a Pauline formation, although there are one or two Hellenistic usages which suggest a basis for it. For St Paul, in any case, " grace " means a Divine force or influence, springing from the disposition of God, and touching human experience. The central explanation is to be found in the coming of Jesus, the Saviour, to the world. Through that, men have learnt for the first time unmistakably, that God's chief attitude to them is that of generous Giver. Of course such a conception had been constantly emphasised, not only in the Old Testament, but also in philosophical discussions.[1] But the gift of Jesus Christ and all that is involved in it supplies a proof such as had never been dreamed of. And the nature of His message, reflecting as it does His experience of God, makes more and more clear this aspect of the Divine. That is to say, men are compassed about by the atmosphere of the Divine generosity. Throughout their ordinary lives, forces are working to lift and perfect them, which God Himself has set in motion. At every turn they are exposed to gracious influences which are meant to be decisive.

[1] Compare the remarkable prominence of the Grace of God in the writings of Philo.

This is what the New Testament writers,
adopting a Jewish term, call their "election."
The primary feature of that idea, *e.g.* for St
Paul, does not possess the arbitrary or capricious
character which is so frequently assigned to
it. It really means God's highest interest in
a man's true prosperity, and the care He lavishes
on the man's salvation. From this the Apostle
always seems to draw the inference that a
career in which God is thus interested can
never fail : that in spite of seeming flaws and
even disobedience, the victorious conclusion
of such a life is pledged by the attitude of God
Himself. There is further the Divine preparation of the soul for worthier things. That
includes the events which have gone to shape
the career, the experiences which have been
the means of its deepest education, the critical
moments when it has made its chief decisions.
There is the call that comes from above when
the life is ready : a direct appeal from God
to man. It may, of course, be clothed in the
garb of some outward event or circumstance.
It is none the less a summons to take one's
place on the right side : to break with the
kingdom of evil and to identify one's self with
the kingdom of God. Finally, there is the
preserving power which guards the God-
directed life, coming to its help in hours of
danger, and vindicating the best tendencies of
the soul against all their enemies. Nothing
brought greater comfort to the Apostle than

this experience : "I am fully persuaded," he writes to the Philippians (i. 6), "that he who began in you his good work will have it accomplished for the day of Christ Jesus."

All such convictions have their fundamental source in the assurance of the Grace of God. Observe what this meant for the early community, especially for those who had joined it from the Pagan world. They have truly passed out of darkness into light. They fully understand what St Paul means when he gives thanks to God because "he translated [us] into the kingdom of the Son of his love " (Col. i. 13). It is the exchange of a tyrannical yoke for one that is gladdening. They need have no concern any longer with the thought of dark and evil powers surrounding them. They can dismiss the idea of inscrutable Fate or incalculable Chance as the supreme deities. They can feel independent of the heavenly bodies and the spirits by which these are believed to be swayed. They can take up with heart and soul the triumphant position of the Apostle, when he exclaims : "Who shall separate us from the love of Christ ? Shall tribulation or straits, or persecution, or famine, or nakedness, or peril, or sword ? . . . I am persuaded that neither death, nor life, nor angels, nor principalities, nor things present, nor things to come, nor power of the height or the depth, nor any other creature, shall be able to separate us

from the love of God, which is in Christ Jesus
our Lord " (Rom. viii. 35, 38–39).

Now this is the entrance of a momentous
force into human affairs. It implies the transformation of religion. It includes a genuine
advance in civilisation. Above all else, it
supplies a sustaining power in the affairs of
every day. No wonder that the calmness and
composure of Christian martyrs, frail old men,
delicate women, and inexperienced boys both
astonished and provoked their persecutors.
These Christians were in possession of a secret
of which the others knew nothing. It was a
futile conflict with the Power which ordered all
things. (For the good and bad effects of persecution, see Harnack, op. cit. i. pp. 487 ff.)

The new type of existence might readily
instigate to pride. As we shall see, this was
a serious result among certain sections of the
community. Those, however, who remained
sensitive to the influences of which I have
spoken, identified themselves with St Paul's
position : " By the grace of God I am what I
am (1 Cor. xv. 10). Every mouth must be
closed in His holy presence " (1 Cor. 1. 29–31).

Note XI

The Fulness of the Time.

One of St Paul's most remarkable phrases is
" the fulness of the time " (Gal. iv. 4). It is
perhaps worth while to linger for a moment

upon the wide range of its significance. For the coming of Jesus with His particular message at one special moment in the process of human development has nothing casual about it. It fits the hour as it could have fitted no other. The time was fully ripe.

On the one hand, the religion of Judaism was ready to pass into a higher stage. The prophets had done their work. They had proclaimed the real nature of God, having discovered Him in their own experience as righteous, holy, and loving. The law had achieved its function. It had impressed upon the people their obligation to holiness which was really obedience to the Divine will. But, unfortunately, it had included in holiness a multitude of observances and enactments which had no necessarily religious bearing at all. And these observances constituted a burdensome yoke for many. Yet they were bound up with the Messianic hopes of the people. These, indeed, depended on the obedience of the nation. This religion of obedience naturally became subject to the motive of fear, and many sensitive consciences shuddered as they thought of the impression of their sinful lives upon an all-holy God. It had become a burning question: How can a man be right with God ?

A devout strain in Judaism had found expression in the Apocalypses. These visions mainly pictured that wonderful future in which the age-long hopes of Israel should be fulfilled :

the kingdom of God should be established among men whether on this earth or a transformed world, by the instrumentality of God Himself or His Messiah : and the chosen people should be vindicated at the cost of the destruction of their enemies. But the Pagan world also was yearning for closer fellowship with the Divine, indeed for salvation ($\sigma\omega\tau\eta\rho\iota\alpha$). We know that in the general dissolution of the ancestral state-religions, the more spiritual philosophy of the time, and, above all, the mystery-cults from the East, appealed to individuals with a new power. In these cults was offered the opportunity of fellowship with a God who endured death, and manifested himself as alive again to those who were ready to acknowledge him. This fellowship involved the promise of immortality.

Moreover, the more earnest Stoics were specially concerned with the furtherance of the moral life. There had been a marked reaction against the earlier laxity. This seems to have prevailed throughout the Roman Empire. It might almost be said that the craving for morality was anticipating that for religion, although, no doubt, the former was really a symptom of the latter. The attachment of many earnest Gentiles by a loose kind of bond to the synagogue was a sign in itself of the worth they assigned to the conceptions of monotheism, of a self-controlled life, of a final retribution on ethical lines. Plainly, the way was being prepared for the perfected stages of revelation in Jesus Christ.

QUESTIONS FOR DISCUSSION.

1. What did St Paul mean by " the grace of God " ?
2. Discuss the meaning of " election."
3. What is meant by " the fulness of the time " ?
4. What is the effect of faith on daily life ?

FOR FURTHER READING.

The Theology of the Epistles, pp. 91–96. By H. A. A. Kennedy.

CHAPTER X

Rom. xii. ; Acts xiii., xiv., xvii. ; John i. 1-18 ; 1 John i.

THE preceding discussion has shown that
Jesus came in " the fulness of the time." The
Apostles, although they would be the last to
minimise the freeness of the Divine working,
were filled with the conviction that the conditions of the age favoured their missionary
enterprise. Let us consider the lines on which
the primary needs of the men and women of
that age were satisfied in the Gospel.

Any acquaintance with the literature of the
Græco-Roman world in the epoch with which
we are concerned reveals the existence of a
craving for moral reformation. The writings of
Seneca, for example, who may be regarded
as an adequate mirror of popular philosophy
on its Stoic side, testify to this on almost every
page. Some of his experiences have, I think,
been interpreted in too profound a sense, but
his general standpoint affords clear enough
evidence. Civilisation had been advancing.
The ethical effect of philosophical teachers
and travelling lecturers, themselves a forcible
argument, was producing fruit all over the
empire. The ruthlessness of civil war had

left a deep impression on sensitive minds.
People of intelligence could easily discern that
the low standard of conduct was seriously
affecting every sphere of life. The Stoic ideal
of the Wise Man probably made a wider appeal
than we usually imagine. There was, in all
likelihood, a good deal of artificiality in this
movement, but it was free from being devoid
of reality. The sharp antithesis between Greek
and barbarian had been toned down. The
world was rapidly becoming unified. Men were
coming to understand their fellows better.
Hence we are not surprised at the emergence
of the conception of " humanity " (*humanitas*),
which might almost be paraphrased, " the
recognition of the worth of mankind," and
soon developed as cognate meanings those of
" gentleness " and " humaneness." It must
be admitted that the conception for long remained largely abstract. Men still shrank from
strangers and enemies. The classical estimates,
e.g. of the Jews, are an irrefutable witness to
prejudice. Nevertheless, the feeling of brotherhood slowly came to be " in the air " ; it
might remain little more than an ideal. But
it belonged to a type of thought which directed
reflective minds to the idea of mutual obligations
and the worth of man as man. In the Stoic
writings especially, noble moral ideals meet
us continually. No doubt these have their
glaring defects. Yet in an age of luxury and
self-indulgence, of secular aims and crass

egoism, we need scarcely be astonished at the fierce attacks upon the passions. Men exhibited themselves so flagrantly as mere slaves of the emotional life that it was no wonder that serious thinkers taught the duty of vanquishing or even extirpating the "passionate" element in the inner being. This reaction, therefore, took extreme forms. And those who could see the good in it doubtless longed for a more balanced expression of what they felt to be of priceless value.

But here we come upon the central flaw in the higher ancient movements. The Stoic morality had noteworthy powers of depicting what they believed to be best. The insuperable difficulty lay in attaining to it. Of course this difficulty attends all moral effort. Christianity conquered Stoicism because it *did* bind its adherents to a higher level of conduct. The influence of this achievement can scarcely be over-estimated. Harnack does not exaggerate when he says : "The entire labour of the Christian mission might be described as a *moral* enterprise, as the awakening and strengthening of the moral sense." And he does justice to the facts in stating that "amid all the convulsions of the soul and body produced by the preaching of a judgment which was imminent, and amid the raptures excited by the Spirit of Christ, morality advanced to a position of greater . purity and security " (*op. cit.* I. pp. 206, 207). Justin Martyr, a

convert from Paganism, declares (*Apol.* ii. 12)
that the steadfastness of Christians convinced
him of their purity, and that these impressions
proved decisive in bringing him over to the faith
(referred to by Harnack, *op. cit.* p. 210).

Closely akin to this consideration is the
further one that in the new faith, religion
and morality were indissolubly fused together.
For us it is, of course, a truism. We in-
stinctively adopt the Master's test : " By their
fruits ye shall know them " (Matt. vii. 11).
A profession of faith is worthless which does
not issue in worthy deeds. But in ancient
religion no such organic connexion between
creed and character was looked for. Indeed,
the spiritual education of the people of Israel
who advanced to so high a morality, largely
consisted in training them to believe that the
essential thing in God is *character*; that He
is holiness, righteousness, love. It meant
much patient discipline before Israel recognised
that God had delight in mercy rather than
sacrifice (Hosea vi. 6). But multitudes in the
Græco-Roman world were ready for this stage
of truth. The profounder thinkers had cast
scorn upon the elaborate rituals of the older
State-cults. They were prepared to welcome
such epoch-making utterances as that of the
prophet Micah : " What doth the Lord require of thee, but to do justly, and to love
mercy, and to walk humbly with thy God "
(vi. 8). These fundamental ethical principles

would appear to many to be self-evident. But
the majority were too definitely accustomed to
the restrictions of time-honoured sanctions to
be able to accept them freely. In the early
society, their highest inclinations were rein-
forced by the authority and example of Jesus
Christ. At this era there is good reason for
saying that a new revelation was hailed rather
than suspected by a great mass of people.
The famous oracles had to some extent lost
their prestige. Even the most devout idolaters
were, to a large extent, transferring their
homage to less prominent deities. It is far
from being true that Paganism was in the
throes of dissolution. The first and immediately succeeding centuries rather witnessed
a heathen revival. The world was at peace.
The Imperial ruler was acclaimed in many
quarters. The worship of the deified
Emperors [1] attained far-reaching influence.
The continuous influx of new cults from the
East increased the influence of Paganism. But
the higher ideas, of which I have spoken, were
in circulation and no artificial measures can
re-create the atmosphere. It is breathed by
every one who possesses vitality. For centuries
the leading thinkers of Pagan humanity had
speculated on the gods who had made the
world, and who superintended the destinies
of mankind. For centuries research had been
devoted to the problem of the relation of God

[1] See Note XI., p. 135.

or the gods to men. In our epoch such research had nearly reached its climax. How
can God enter into contact with His creatures ?
Can He reveal Himself to the souls that thirst
after Him ? Is He too great and exalted to
have any dealings with weak and burdened
mortals ? Many answered : " God is completely transcendent : He is infinitely distant
from an evil world : He cannot in any way
touch the material." But even some of these
answerers were sure that God must reveal Himself : must come to the help of frail mortals :
must show forth those qualities in His character
which can encourage and raise men into His
presence. For He and His creatures are akin.
Humanity is separated from the animal world
by that endowment with reason, which is
really a spark of the Divine nature.

Hence the category of mediation becomes
very prominent. It had long been familiar
to men's minds in very different environments
and in very divergent forms. Moses, Attis,
Adonis—all these might be adduced as in one
sense or other mediating forces. And then
there were the semi-personified abstractions—
Wisdom, Nous ($\nu o \hat{v} \varsigma$), Logos, all of them real
mediators and penetrating deep into the requirements of human thought. But Jesus
Christ met the want in a manner that was
all-surpassing. The Divinity of the living
Lord was the common confession of the early
community. He spoke with the authority of

God behind Him. But He had lived a human life, with which His followers were intimately acquainted, so they could never conceive Him as an abstraction. They remembered the tone of His voice, the appearance of His person, His very questions. His had been a full and genuine mediation in the days of His flesh. He had taught as one having authority and not as the scribes. Their impression of Him had transformed their lives. Not least, their impression of the living Christ. For in His exalted condition they felt nearer to Him than ever. And His presence *was* more real to them through the gift of the Holy Spirit. That was the most compelling form His mediation assumed. Their sense of fresh, spiritual power was even more wonderful than their apprehension of Jesus' teaching or their admiration of His character.

Now, the phenomena amid which they moved, forced the members of the early community to come to various important conclusions regarding Jesus. Some of these are handed down to us in the Epistles of St Paul, and we cannot be sure how far they represent a wide circle of believers.

It is not surprising to find that for St Paul, Christ is the image (εἰκών) of God, a description which would be difficult to distinguish from that of the Fourth Gospel, the Logos or " rational word " of God. The background of the idea is both Jewish and Greek. The Jews were not attracted to philosophising. Yet a time inevitably came in their religious thought when they closely approached it. Their Wisdom-literature,[1] it is true, consists for the most part of a practical application of moral principles to the ordinary details of life, but every here and there a deeper strain appears, urged on the authors by the more profound problems of existence. Such a strain is noteworthy in Prov. viii. 22–36, where Wisdom appears as the personification of the Divine reason, God's instrument in the creation of the world and of men. Similarly, in the later *Wisdom of Solomon*, vii. 22—viii. 4, wisdom is called " an unspotted mirror of the working of God, and an image ($\epsilon i\kappa \acute{\omega}\nu$) of his goodness " (ver. 26). In the *Wisdom of the Son of Sirach* (called Ecclesiasticus in the LXX.) there occurs in chap. iv. 3–9, an interesting parallel to the passages already quoted. Similar passages occur in the writings of the famous Jewish thinker of Alexandria, Philo, but far more often than Wisdom the Logos is the centre of them. That reminds us that the all-pervading Reason of the Stoics has richly contributed to the conception under our consideration. And the result (which is also the logical climax of St Paul's standpoint in Coloss. i. 15–19), is the Logos of chap. i. of the Fourth Gospel. These are far from being empty speculations of the leading disciples of Jesus. They are deductions

[1] See Note XIII., *Jewish Wisdom and Literature.*

from what they discovered of Him in their
religious experiences clothed in the thought-
forms of their day. It may be hard for us to
assimilate them, but if we cannot, we must
find some substitute.

We may be sure that they represent profoundly real and satisfying thoughts for these
early believers. Here is how God has chosen
to make His will known. There is nothing
vague about the method, because it is in Him
Who is His image. Probably this idea would
appeal more directly to Pagans than to anyone else. They would be familiar with its
earlier use. They would soon come to realise
how readily the features of Jesus could group
themselves within it. And it brought to them
the intellectual kind of satisfaction for which
their minds were craving. One has little
doubt that the fitness of Jesus for the function
of Revealer formed one of the most influential
powers in early Christianity.

Both in the Old Testament and in the profounder strata of Greek religious aspiration,
the aim of religion was depicted as nothing
less than fellowship with God. The argument
of the Epistle to the Hebrews reminds us of
the pains taken to justify that need to the
consciousness of some faltering Christians.
If this goal be attained everything is accomplished. The ardour of the aspiration seems
to have steadily increased among the more
religious minds in Pagan society. All sorts of

instruments, good and bad, were used to achieve the end. Fellowship with God was conceived in the most divergent fashion, embracing the crudest as well as the most spiritual solutions. The most spiritual of all was the way recognised in the early Christian community. Faith, as they were led to understand it, remained for long more or less free from superstitious elements. It was the movement of the entire inner being towards the exalted Christ, and it was He Who opened the path for men to God. No doubt the author of 1 John represents a universally recognised position within the society. "He that acknowledgeth the Son hath the Father also " (ii. 23).

It is unnecessary to refer to New Testament or early Patristic references which confirm this point of view. They are the rule rather than the exception. And they bring into prominence the satisfaction of that need which was everywhere felt. Those who became convinced that they could actually find God apart from mere ritual or magical processes, must have been thrilled by a sense of new religious mastery. It would become one of the fascinations of the early Christian Gospel that it promised to remove all the barriers between men's souls and God.

I am not sure how far St Paul's view of the Atonement illuminated for darkened hearts the genuine way to God. For many minds it would be decisive. Indeed, this circle of thought requires careful consideration for our epoch.

It has often been pointed out that one of the most remarkable religious revivals of our period was associated with the worship of Asclepius, the god of healing. We know how many people, both men and women, burdened with distressed lives, had recourse to his sanctuaries, where they betook themselves to sleep, with the expectation of receiving revelations from the god during their slumber. The cult of Asclepius became diffused in every direction, and the god received the two highly significant titles of " Saviour " ($\sigma\omega\tau\dot{\eta}\rho$) and " warm friend of man " ($\phi\iota\lambda\alpha\nu\theta\rho\omega\pi\acute{o}\tau\alpha\tau\sigma$). In fact " healing " came to be one of the chief desiderata of sin-sick souls. And in these cases, as is natural, it is often difficult to distinguish between disease of body and disease of soul. Now the Gospels had depicted Jesus as the Good Physician. Such a passage as Mark ii. 3–12 shows how flexible was the boundary between the physical and the spiritual. This accords with the modern conception of their unity. Hence the new life which the living Lord inspired came to be regarded pre-eminently as a life of *health*. It is very remarkable that the famous Church historian, Eusebius, in describing Jesus as physician (H.E. x. 4, 11), quotes verbatim from an ancient medical treatise, Pseudo-

Hippocrates on *Flatulence* (referred to by Harnack, *op. cit.* p. 106, n. 2).

But the most notable fact in the new religion is the audience to which it appeals. Older faiths were intended for the pure and the healthy Thus, Celsus, the strong Anti-Christian, says (Origen, *c. Cels.* iii. 69 f.) : "Those who invite people to participate in other solemnities, make the following proclamation, 'He who hath clean hands or sensible spirit (is to draw near),' or, again, 'He who is pure from all stain, conscious of no sin in his soul, and living an honourable and just life (may approach),' . . . But let us now hear what sort of people those Christians invite. 'Anyone who is a sinner,' they say, ' or foolish, or simple-minded '— in short, any unfortunate will be accepted by the Kingdom of God." "Here," as Harnack aptly says, "Celsus has sketched as lucidly as one could desire, the cardinal differences between Christianity and ancient religion" (*op. cit.* p. 104). Jesus Himself had said : "I came not to call righteous people but sinners " (Mark ii. 17). The carrying out of His intention lay at the heart of the early community. It was its glory and its privilege to be faithful to the Master. This was a proclamation of new hope and new life to many restless and tormented souls. In the epoch which we are considering just as truly as in Jesus' lifetime the scornful criti-

cism of the Pharisees proved a genuine
Gospel : " This man receiveth sinners " (Luke
xv. 2).

Note XII

Emperor Worship

We know from the Apocalypse that one of
the bitterest foes which confronted Christianity
in the early centuries was Emperor-worship.
In that enigmatic book it is symbolised by
the Beast which comes up out of the sea.
The second Beast represents the provincial
priesthood of the imperial cult, which had
attained enormous power in Asia Minor. In
Eastern civilisations like those of Babylon,
Persia, and Egypt, the king, from an early
time, was regarded as the son of a god. In
the Greek world probably the nearest approach
to this circle of ideas was the super-human
honour paid to men, who, while living, had
been pre-eminent for some remarkable characteristic which had profoundly impressed
their fellows. These two currents of thought
were sure to intermingle when the conquering
genius of Alexander the Great brought East
and West together in a common Hellenism.
As a matter of fact, the deification of rulers
takes very definite shape in the kingdoms of
Alexander's successors. A step of unique
significance for history was taken when divine
titles were given to Roman rulers. The custom

seems to have begun in Asiatic communities, in the last century of the Republic, when temples were erected to Roman proconsuls and generals. This was partly due to the cringing adulation characteristic of Eastern races, and partly to real gratitude for the stability of Roman supremacy. For a time Augustus restricted the worship of Roman citizens to the deified Julius, his uncle, but accepted divine honours for himself only from his Græco-Asiatic subjects. The first temple dedicated to his worship seems to have been one at Pergamon, erected to " Rome and Augustus." Henceforward divine honours were heaped upon Augustus in his Eastern dominions. At a later period he accepted deification even from Italian communities, *e.g.* from Beneventum (about 14 B.C.).

The name κύριος, Lord, so regularly applied to Jesus Christ in the Apostolic Church, was constantly used of the deified emperors. Thus, in a decree of a town in Bœotia in honour of Nero, he is called, " Lord of the whole world." What intensifies the significance of the situation for the New Testament is that the epithet " our Lord " is often attached to the name of emperors in Greek inscriptions.

It may be said that Emperor-worship unified the state religion. It is easy to picture the impression made on the inhabitants of the Roman provinces as they listened to the Christian missionaries heaping on the Founder

of the faith the highest titles which adorned
the imperial ruler, that ruler whose worship
was the most important symbol of all that
they valued in their political life.

Note XIII

Jewish Wisdom-Literature

This literature which may be said to enshrine
the philosophy of Judaism is noteworthy for
its practical problems. Generally, it does not
touch metaphysics at all. When it does, its
interest is still in the problem of conduct. I
would include under the above heading Job,
Proverbs, Ecclesiastes, the Wisdom of Solomon,
and the Wisdom of the Son of Sirach,
designated in the Apocrypha, Ecclesiasticus.
To judge, *e.g.* by the Epistles of Paul, its influence seems to have extended as the years went
on. Possibly the Hellenistic colouring which
attached itself to some parts pushed it into
more marked prominence. It is characterised
for the most part by sanity of judgment and
persistent ethical interest. Its central conception of wisdom has the capacity of being
adapted to needs which made themselves felt
in the first century A.D. When men were
groping after the idea of adequate mediation
between God and the world, this semi-personified conception served with delicacy to express
a relationship which did not require to be too

sharply formulated. It was no small advantage for men of Jewish blood to be able to point to a category in their literature which could challenge comparison with the Logos of Greek thought. Perhaps this conception took a far larger place in early Christian thought than we are apt to imagine. Certainly some of the most obscure utterances of St Paul find a clearer explanation in this direction than in any other. Possibly Dr Rendel Harris is justified in supposing that the equation of Christ with the Eternal Wisdom ($\sigma o\phi i a$) of God had an unusual influence both in moulding the Pauline thought and that of the early Church Fathers. It will always, however, be a moot question whether the Hellenistic conception of mediating Forces, as in Philo, or the Wisdom-category made the strongest impact on the mind of the great Apostle of the Gentiles.

QUESTIONS FOR DISCUSSION.

1. How is Christianity better than Stoicism ?
2. What did the early Church mean by calling Jesus " Saviour " ?
3. What needs of the soul are met by Jesus Christ ?
4. What characteristic most clearly differentiates Christianity from Pagan religions ?
5. How does Christianity satisfy the desire for fellowship with God ?

FOR FURTHER READING.

The Open Light. By N. Micklem.
Hibbert Lectures, pp. 139–170. By E. Hatch.

CHAPTER XI

1 John iii. ; James i., ii., iii., iv., v.

LIKE all vital societies, the early Christian community was from the outset subject to remarkable laws of growth. It is comparatively futile to start with a scheme of the probable lines on which such a community should develop. That will mean the attempt to crush living forces within an artificial framework. We are more likely to arrive at truth if we try obediently to follow the facts, arranging them for convenience' sake under certain broad categories, which do not profess to exhaust the various lines of evolution, but rather to explain the general drift. As the years went on, it was inevitable that the manifold implications of Christian faith and conduct should reveal themselves, and that they should tend to assume stereotyped forms. For human nature, even when touched by Divine influence, is not infinitely original. It is fond of repeating itself, that is, of experimenting with familiar courses. I need scarcely say that all this belongs to unconscious effort.

(a) We have seen that essential to the message of Jesus is the thought that " God is a spirit and they that worship Him must worship Him in spirit and in truth." This great conception never falls into abeyance. It may be overshadowed by superficial ideas, it may be contaminated by Pagan formalism or magic, it may be spun out into thin abstractions. But it survives as the hall-mark of the mind of Jesus. St Paul was always alive to the identity of spirituality with true religion, and the entire force of his testimony told on its behalf. There can be little doubt that one of his chief tasks was to preserve this element alive. For among immature converts from Paganism it was always exposed to danger; and he knew that the future of Christianity was bound up with its endurance.

Now the evidence of the sub-Apostolic writings reveals a glaring declension from St Paul. The enthusiasm of the earlier days had vanished, as it was bound to do. Second and third generations had arisen who, on the whole, had received the Christian tradition at second-hand. I do not at all mean that their faith was a perversion. But many of its profoundest elements were not prominent. There is always the tendency to accommodate your religion to the surrounding atmosphere. In this case it may truly be said that the atmosphere was eclectic, and as such, characteristic of the thought of the period.

But St Paul had penetrated once for all to the secret of Jesus. He had, on the basis of

experience, emphasised the central features of
Jesus' Gospel. That emphasis could never
be ignored. It was caught up by the deeper
minds in the community and adjusted to the
ever-changing environment.

The relation to St Paul's teaching of the
writer of the Fourth Gospel has never been
adequately discussed. But a glance at the
latter makes clear how far-reaching it has been.
I do not for a moment suggest that " John "
has been so impressed by his brother-Apostle
that he feels he cannot do better than develop
his standpoint. But he has steeped himself
in the Pauline Epistles, and he is familiar with
the great missionary's mode of preaching
Christ. As the result of his own reflection on
his Master's gospel, viewed in the light of his
changing experience, he has discerned the
risks to which the Christian message is peculiarly liable. In the Greek world, ideas completely overshadowed facts for the more
thoughtful. Bare history was regarded as to
a large extent external. Penetrating minds
professed to view it as the husk of a kernel.
Many were ready to approach it as primarily
symbolic. Such a tendency had been long
afloat. We may most conveniently refer to
Philo of Alexandria as illustrating how the
Old Testament narratives might be viewed by
a devout man, who was loyally attached to the
conception of their value as Divine revelations.
Unless with deliberate resolution we try to

identify ourselves with the mental habits of the period, we cannot hope to reach solutions of its most perplexing problems.

Now when the Fourth Gospel was composed, a variety of disintegrating influences were asserting themselves. People were entering the Christian community who had been profoundly affected by the drift of Hellenistic philosophy and religion. The very vagueness of their own position had exposed them to the impact of plausible views from all directions. On these they were apt to pride themselves, especially if they could fit them in to their supreme quest, the knowledge of God. Preeminent in this group were those whom, for convenience' sake, we may call Gnostics, without stopping to attempt any precise definition of the term. Although, as we have noted, knowledge must chiefly mean for them something practical and experimental, the philosophical cast of outlook which many of them favoured was bound to exalt the intellectual elements in experience. Their views became more and more subjective. They loved to move among abstractions. The data of historical experience ceased to appeal to them. The figure of Jesus of Nazareth stood far away. Tradition was flexible. It was almost inevitable that they should abstract from the actual Person and concentrate on those aspects of His message which coincided with this general standpoint. Hence they were disposed to group Jesus Christ with those various media through whom God had revealed Himself to men. Curiously enough, some of the great Pauline conceptions could without difficulty be adapted to their inclinations, more especially those that sprang from the central fact of Christian living, the possession of the Holy Spirit. This endowment could be exaggerated to mean liberation from everything earthly or belonging to the time-process. They professed independence of the life of sense, although that life asserted itself among them at the cost of ordinary morality. They were the "spiritual" people ($\pi\nu\epsilon\upsilon\mu\alpha\tau\iota\kappa\circ\iota\varsigma$), already as good as Divine, raised above all the common sanctions, infallible in the matters of the higher life, and so, absolved from the demand of regulating the lower. That is, roughly speaking, the kind of situation which is faced in the Fourth Gospel and the Johannine Epistles. These "Gnostics" are to a considerable extent Jews, or highly sympathetic, at many points, with Jewish traditions, although some of the most famous are bitterly opposed to the Jewish position, going the length of distinguishing, on the dim basis of very ancient speculation, between the good God, Who has spoken to men in Jesus of Nazareth, and the Demiurge or Creator, an imperfect Being, who created the evil material world, and was closely associated with the fortunes of the people of Israel. The writer of the above-mentioned

books, to whom we shall give for convenience'
sake the traditional name " John," was peculiarly fitted to grapple with such positions.
He was profoundly at home in the Old Testament, a sincere champion of its deepest truth.
He was in close touch with the prevailing
currents of thought in the Hellenistic world,
and valued what was best in their aspirations.
But, above all, his soul had been laid hold of
by the revelation in Jesus Christ. As a loyal
Jew, he had welcomed the appearance of the
true Messiah. Far more, He had come to
know the heart and mind and life of Jesus,
not merely as the Master had walked in Galilee
and Judæa, but as He abode in the unseen
world, and came into living fellowship with
His faithful followers. He regarded the career
of Jesus *sub specie æternitatis*, unaffected by
the change of outward events, a manifestation
of God's gracious purpose of love and life for
His children. He did not rely on memories ;
although these counted for much. He was
always in touch with the Exalted Lord. But
that Lord was no mere bundle of attributes,
no merely religious ideal. He was Jesus of
Nazareth, Who had passed through human
life, not as a phantom (so the Gnostics held),
but as a real man who mingled with His fellow-
creatures in joy and sorrow, knew pain and
weariness and grief, drew round Him a band
of congenial companions, was contradicted,
scorned, misunderstood. " John " indeed

could bear witness to important historical traditions of the Master, which he recorded with the Synoptic Gospels before him, sometimes using these traditions to supplement or correct the earlier Gospels, at others adapting them to suit his large general purpose.

It is probably impossible to overestimate the service done to early Christianity by the production of the Fourth Gospel. Just because it appeared at a time when sketches of the life of Jesus were in busy circulation ; just because it emphasised the indissoluble connexion between the historical and the exalted Christ ; just because it made plain the unique importance of the spirituality of His career and His message ; just because it made men realise that, although the first witnesses of the Lord had passed, He was as real as ever, nay, more real than ever through the power of His Holy Spirit, it came as an immense illumination to the early Church.

It put a mighty weapon into the hands of those who, while they had not seen, had yet believed, against their subtle opponents who professed to despise the visible world and its events, and, with a bitter contempt for their brethren, to assert their own superiority. The supreme message of the Love of God was the cementing influence in the Christian community. That love was nothing vague or general. It went forth to living individuals and their concerns. And it could be understood by them because it had been embodied in One Who served among them as their Brother. Faith and love may be called the *foci* of the Johannine writings. No forces were more calculated to preserve from corruption those men and women who had identified themselves with Christ. The whole of their pressure lay in the direction of the inward and the spiritual. So that we are not surprised to find in these documents that the more or less material pictures of the more primitive belief have yielded to a process belonging to a sphere in which time and space have no importance.

(*b*) The careful reader, however, will discover in " John " no less than in St Paul the germs of subsequent doctrine. As soon as a society begins to be organised and consolidated, its leaders and its members must gradually agree, first informally, then by more or less regular steps, upon their common profession of faith. Much of importance may be left in the background, but there will be certain positions which really justify the establishment of the new corporation. Hints of this occur throughout the New Testament. The process is, of course, accelerated by developments which challenge the original essentials. The Person and achievement of Jesus Christ, the relation of the believers to God and to the world, the means of coming into touch with the Divine, the source of authority in religion (in the various

forms which this discussion assumed)—these
will clamour for a certain amount of definition,
and the agreement reached will react on the
whole question of the administration of the
society.

We have observed how eagerly the ancient
mind grasped at rules. So we are thoroughly
prepared for a period when the more flexible
and living growth yields to stereotyped forms
and combinations. The forms need not be
predominantly doctrinal. For doctrine constantly finds expression in conduct. Throughout the later New Testament writings, the
chief stress seems to be laid on " good works."
We understand the situation, for, as has been
noted, the mature stages of a religious movement will inevitably be occupied with the
moral standard of action. That is a sign of
health and vitality. But it is significant how
often in the *Pastoral Epistles* " good works "
are associated with " sound doctrine." It is
altogether praiseworthy that high ethical
activity should be the issue of religious association. But there is an easy descent from such
a position into the other, that, namely, of
identifying religion with the performance of
certain definite services to God. Gradually,
the position will be taken up that fellowship
with God is the consequence of certain recognised efforts, no doubt worthy in their
character, which depend on the resolute determination of the Christian. This will cut the

nerve of truly religious action, which is reliance on the Divine Grace and that sympathy, which is attained through faith, with the self-sacrifice and the redeeming power of the living Christ. It will be ultimately the parent of those doctrines which involve counsels of perfection and the higher religious status of a class which offers for exceptional service, and which prompt to courses like the "doing of penance," the embracing of certain unique vows, the undertaking of a regulated number of approved "duties." It really means the antithesis of St Paul's famous injunction : "Work out your own salvation with fear and trembling, for it is God who is working in you" (Phil. ii. 12, 13). Hence spring monastic ideals and orders claiming a peculiar attainment of piety which deserves, or rather, has the right to a special type of reward.

As soon as this conception becomes influential, the centre of gravity is shifted from the inward to the external. For religious activity which is not in direct touch with God is bound to become mechanical or superficial. Accordingly, matters of organisation and arrangement begin to overshadow spiritual aspirations. The *Pastoral Epistles* provide examples of what I mean, in its germination. In these documents we find many echoes, and impressive echoes, of the earlier type of experimental piety. But we are here on the threshold of the epoch of rules and regulations. The "New Law" has come into operation. And the circumstances of the situation will inevitably favour its development into endless minutiæ. This tendency to externalism will speedily induce an emphasis on ceremonial, alien to the spirituality of the New Testament. I do not venture to say that there was no use in such developments. Many immature minds, scarcely alive to the central forces inherent in Christianity, with obscure notions of the spirit or spiritual freedom, would crave for continual direction both as to belief and as to duty. Many childish imaginations would at first miss the pomp and colour to which they had been accustomed in other religions, and the demand, as invariably, would tend to create the supply. And each one of these influences would lead to the thinning down of the great spiritual ideas which men like St Paul and " St John " uttered from the depths of their own religious experience.

(c) I have not yet referred to an all-important feature of the situation, what one may call the *average* Christianity of the period. Obviously such a question will be the hardest to deal with, as it implies a knowledge of documents which we cannot claim to possess. Here, indeed, we must form our estimate under the guidance of our experience of later Church life, trying to avoid all dogmatism and to express our opinions with due caution.

A question which has for long interested New Testament students, although it has

never been made the subject of thorough
discussion, relates to the *extent* to which St Paul
was understood by the communities with which
he corresponded. The controversies to which
his teaching, all through the centuries, has
given rise, rather suggest that only a select
number of Christians can have fathomed the
profundities of his spiritual instruction. Of
course, we must remember that his corre-
spondents were fully acquainted with the
circumstances of the situations which prompted
the direction of his utterances. His missionary
preaching had certainly convinced the minds
and hearts of multitudes, for they had surrendered themselves to Jesus Christ. One
ventures to think that his Epistles took a
wider scope, and trusted to the illumination of
the Spirit to open the minds of the readers to
those vistas of truth which the great Apostle
himself discerned. But when St Paul had
passed away, and Christianity was no longer
a novelty, received with enthusiasm, a con-
ventional tone must have invaded the community. There would still be abundance of
spiritual life and abundance of opportunities
for realising it. But there would also be many
minds of an ordinary type within the community, either by choice or by birth, which,
while appreciating the value of the revelation
of God which had reached them in Christ,
would begin to accept that revelation as a
matter of course, and being without vision to

grasp all its implications would be content to apply its leading principles to their thought and conduct. Such application would, of course, fix their behaviour at a level high above the average, but it need not involve a specially deep experience, and they might be quite satisfied to be loyal to that which they had been taught. In many cases, their convictions would be largely at second-hand, so they would lack the fiery enthusiasm which characterised a man like St Paul.

Probably we have a picture of this phase of the community in the Epistle of James, which, with many scholars, I regard as a document belonging to the close of the first century. It strikingly represents the prevailing Græco-Roman culture of the time, revealing its acquaintance with Hellenistic thought and usages, reflecting a good deal of the current higher morality, showing numerous points of contact with a cultivated religious thinker like Philo. It is hazardous to attempt to locate the community or communities addressed. They have had a considerable experience of what Christianity means. But the result does not inspire us like the Pauline issues. Their religion is quite alive, and it is not divorced from their social life. But there appears to be a tinge of self-satisfaction about it, and it is considerably mixed up with the claims of ordinary business. Evidently it displays a superficial side. A great number of the Christians addressed are eager and incessant talkers. Their ambition is to be teachers, of one another no doubt, and they have lost control of their tongues. This suggests self-confidence as to religious position, and the desire to exhibit their knowledge. But along-side of it the writer chides the emptiness of their profession. They are fond of repeating the old watchword of faith, but it is apt to be devoid of content. Their religion does not find real expression in action which corresponds. They are well acquainted with strings of moral maxims, but they are prone to strife, hatred, jealousy, servility, and the greed of gain. We have here a very mixed picture, but not more so than we should expect. Christianity proved itself adequate to transform human nature, but it could not recreate communities mechanically. As soon as they began to ignore the Fatherhood of God, the old forces vigorously revived, and the future Kingdom began to appear as remote as ever.

(d) The tendencies at work in the society addressed by James appear in developed form in the life of the second century. There we see clearly that even the best writers, the so-called Apostolic Fathers, fell far short, in their religious counsels, of the standard set by St Paul. Again and again, when they happen to deal with some of his central doctrines, they approach them with uncertainty and reveal a confused notion of their rich content. Perhaps the most influential factor in their thought is the Old Testament : a fact which reminds us of the dominance of its great teachings in the life of the early community. From some of the writers we gain the impression of an alien strain of thought, representing earlier Greek authorities. The process has already begun of adjusting Christian ideas to their environment ; of showing how the Christian position can be buttressed by the opinions of men like Plato and even Homer. This process was destined to advance with ever-increasing scope until Christian writers are found deliberately filling pages of self-defence with arguments drawn from Hellenic writers.

Yet although all this amounts to accommodation to the surrounding atmosphere, it would be rash to call it an irrelevant or futile movement. St Paul himself had said : " I have become all things to all men that in any case I might save some " (1 Cor. ix. 22). Probably it was above all things needful that points of contact should be established between Christianity and Paganism. Such contact must inevitably cut both ways. It served to bring out the reasonableness of Christianity, but sometimes at the cost of its unique character. It paved the way to the understandings of men of a particular type of training, but it would be likely to dishearten those who were craving for a new revelation.

I have attempted to review briefly those

diverging lines of development, whose seeds
were contained in the early community, and
have noted the dangerous potentialities which
some of them involved. But even in the most
superficial phases of the new Faith, the idea
never vanished that the living God *had spoken* :
that the world could never again be as it had
been before : that a high moral responsibility
was laid upon men's consciences by the re-
demptive achievement of Jesus Christ. So
there remained in the hands of the early mission
an instrument " mighty through the Divine
power to pull down strongholds," as the missionaries " cast down reasonings and every
high thing that exalted itself against the
knowledge of God and brought every thought
into captivity to the obedience of Christ "
(2 Cor. x. 4, 5).

From the beginning until now, the Christian
Church has been exposed to peculiar perils.
It has been the butt of criticism at every stage
of its history. Most of the criticism starts
with the assumption that the Church *ought* to
be popular. Surely this is an extraordinary
presupposition, when we realise by experience
that selfishness is the most potent force in
average human nature. The marvel is that
in the apparently darkest ages of Christianity
from the first century up to the present, genuine
Divine life can be traced in the most unlikely
surroundings. All through its history in the
world it has been mainly supported and pro-

pagated by unknown men and women, often simple and diffident, who have had the vision of the glory of Jesus Christ, and for whom that has overshadowed all else besides. Human society is being driven, by hard and ruthless forces, to recognise that the cure of its pain and dissatisfaction is not to be expected from the progress of thought or the advances of science, but from a whole-hearted allegiance to Him Who pleased not Himself, and Who was therefore able to say : "Learn from Me . . . for My yoke is easy and My burden light."

QUESTIONS FOR DISCUSSION.

1. What is the principal value of the Fourth Gospel ?
2. Discuss the use of rules and ritual in Christianity.
3. What dangers especially threaten the period following a religious revival ?

FOR FURTHER READING.

The Word Made Flesh. By Edward Grubb.
History of Christianity in the Apostolic Age, pp. 506–545. By A. C. M'Giffert.

INDEX (*A*)

INDEX (B)

Scripture References

www.ingramcontent.com/pod-product-compliance
Lightning Source LLC
Chambersburg PA
CBHW071445090426
42737CB00011B/1788